Aug 2/08

"The Game is Easy Life is Hard - No Guarantees"
- Fergie Jenkins

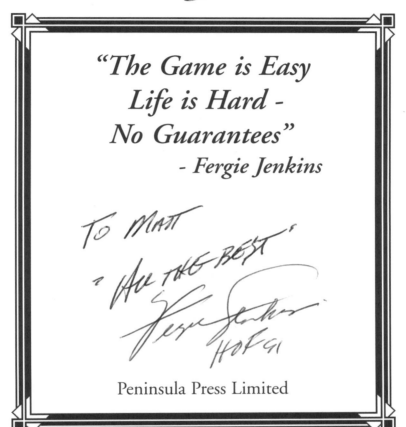

To Matt

" All the Best "

Fergie Jenkins
HOF 91

Peninsula Press Limited

The Game is Easy - Life is Hard

The story of Ferguson Jenkins Jr.

By

Dorothy Turcotte

Published by The Fergie Jenkins Foundation,
Grimsby, Ontario

2003

National Library of Canada Cataloguing in Publication Data

Turcotte, Dorothy, 1929-
The game is easy, life is hard : the story of Ferguson Jenkins

Includes bibliographical references and index.
ISBN 0-9689609-0-1

1. Jenkins, Ferguson, 1943- 2. Baseball players--Canada--
Biography. I. Fergie Jenkins Foundation II. Title.

GV865.J38T87 2002   796.357'092
            C2001-902993-4

ISBN 0-9689609-0-1

Printed by Peninsula Press Limited, 217 Bunting Road, St.
Catharines, Ontario L2M 3Y2

Table of Contents

Introduction

It was late on a Saturday in December, 1996. The gymnasium at the Welland Campus of Niagara College was still crowded with children and their parents. It was the last day of a pitching clinic for young baseball players, and the two celebrity instructors, Scott Bullet and Fergie Jenkins, were signing autographs.

At the back of the line, a man waited patiently by himself. He was not holding a bat, ball or photograph to be autographed. When the last fan carried off his prized memento of the occasion, he approached Fergie and introduced himself as Carl Kovacs.

"I'm chairman of the Grimsby Sports Council," he explained. "We're planning a big celebrity sports dinner next September to raise money for some local charities. It's going to be a big affair, a first-ever in our town, and we'd like you to come as one of our celebrities. Do you think you would be able to make it?"

"Sounds like something I'd like to be involved in," Fergie admitted. "Tell you what. Give me your name and phone number and I'll have my wife, Lydia, give you a call. She arranges all the bookings for me, and she'll know if I'm available on that date." Carl wrote out the information and Fergie slipped it in his pocket. "She'll call you within four weeks, I promise," Fergie assured him.

As Carl walked back to his car, he thought "Seems like a really nice guy. But he's on the road so much, and Christmas will soon be here. They'll be so busy. I'll bet I'll never hear from her."

Carl learned something about Fergie as a result of that first meeting. When Fergie makes a promise, he keeps it. Lydia did not call in four weeks. She called in two weeks. She confirmed that Fergie would be available for the September date, and that he was looking forward to the event. He was the first celebrity to sign up for the Sports Celebrity dinner.

Although neither Carl Kovacs nor Ferguson Jenkins knew it, that meeting was the start of something big.

Delores Jenkins with her 14-month-old son, Ferguson Arthur Jenkins - Jenkins family photo

1. The First Dream

When Ferguson Jenkins was a young lad, he often questioned male relatives about their height. Fergie was growing rapidly, and he wanted to know his prospects for the future. His mother, Dolores, was 5'10" - tall for a woman, and her male relatives were all much taller than that.

So Fergie wanted to know "How tall were you when you were my age?" "When did you stop growing?" "Did you do anything special to get taller?" One summer, he grew three inches. By the age of 14, his shoe size was 12.

Fergie believed that if he reached the height of 6'10", something that his genetic heritage could very well make possible, he could make a career in basketball, a game that he truly loved. As it turned out, he topped out at 6'5", but by then, there were other opportunities on the horizon. The disappointment was not as great as it might have been. Later in life, though, when he had a back problem, Fergie learned that he was born without one of the vertebra in his lower back. If he had had it, he would have been an inch or two taller.

To understand Fergie Jenkins as a person, you need to know something about his family background, for it had a profound influence on every aspect of his life. It was obvious to everyone who knew him, even from an early age, that Ferguson Jenkins had a wonderful, wholesome family life.

One sportswriter referred to Fergie as being born "east of Detroit." That is true, but not accurate. He was born at St. Joseph's Hospital in Chatham, Ontario on December 13th, 1942. His father, Ferguson Sr. was chef at the Holiday Inn in town. He had started out at age 14, making pancakes at the Devonshire and Kenilworth racetracks during the summer months. Later he worked for 13 years as cook on the Great Lakes steamer *Eugene J. Buffington* owned by the Pittsburgh Steam Company. When he was 19, he was the youngest cook on the line, and at that time won an award for bread baking. Fergie Sr. developed into a first-class chef, and was a much sought-after caterer in the Chatham area. He cooked regularly at the Chatham Police Club's Steak Nights, and was made an official lifetime member of the club.

Fergie Sr. loved to cook at home, too, and kept the Jenkins table laden with good things. He especially liked to make pastry and bake bread. Fergie Jr.'s favourite was gingerbread, so the Jenkins home always had the aroma of wonderful things to eat. The entire neighbourhood loved an invitation to the Jenkins house.

Fergie Sr. once described his son's favourite meal, one that he prepared often for the family. It consisted of medium rare prime beef, Yorkshire pudding, baked potato, and tossed salad with thousand island dressing.

"My lemon cream and apple pies are a speciality," Fergie Sr. once said "but I never serve a heavy dessert after a heavy meal."

Born in Windsor, Ontario, Ferguson Sr. came from a family of many excellent cooks who had emigrated from the Bahamas several generations earlier. His father was also named Ferguson, so young Fergie Jr. was the third generation to bear that first name. Sometimes, in later years, he was referred to as "the man with two last names."

The Jenkins family was never poor, because Fergie Sr. always had a good job, either cooking, or at times working as a chauffeur. He drove for several wealthy families in the Chatham area, including the Seagrams at one time. Sometimes, when Fergie Jr. was young, his father would be working in Windsor as a chef. At arranged times, Delores would put Fergie on the train in Chatham, and his father would meet him in Windsor. It was a great treat for both father and son.

Although Fergie Sr. was a kind, smiling man, it was clear to everyone, including Fergie Jr., that he was his son's father, not his best buddy. One stern look from his father told Fergie exactly what was expected of him, and he did it promptly. Fergie Sr. was not a tall man, just 5'9", but he had an air of authority. His son outstripped him in height at an early age, but even before that, Fergie Sr. never used physical punishment on his son. He didn't have to. Because of his paternal and friendly nature, Fergie Sr. was known as "Pops" Jenkins by the entire neighbourhood.

Fergie Jr.'s mother, Dolores, was descended from runaway slaves who had come to the Chatham area via the underground railroad. The underground railroad was a loosely organized system of private citizens who helped fugitive slaves from the American South escape to Canada during the Nineteenth Century. Sympathetic citizens would hide the fugitives until they could be moved to another safe location farther north, until at last they crossed the border to freedom in Canada. One of these slaves, Josiah Henson, escaped in 1830 and founded the Dawn community near Dresden, Upper Canada (now Ontario). About 30,000 slaves escaped to Canada in this way. Southwestern Ontario welcomed many more black families over the years, and there is still a large black population in that area.

Delores Jenkins was a devoted wife and mother who looked forward to having a large family. However, that was not to be. She had a rare eye disease from birth. Her vision was never good, but was not seriously affected until the trauma of a long labour at Fergie Jr.'s birth ruptured her optic nerve and robbed her of sight almost completely. She could watch television by looking at the screen on an angle, using her peripheral vision, but she was legally blind. While the two Fergies watched television, she enjoyed listening to her portable radio.

Although he was an "only child", Fergie was never lonely. Both of his parents attracted friendships and were well known in the community. It was natural that they should also welcome their son's friends into their home.

At first, the Jenkins family lived at 217 Colborne Street in Chatham, sharing a house with Dolores's mother, Cassie Jackson. Although it was a largely black neighbourhood, Fergie quickly made friends with the other children, both black and white. It was in this neighbourhood that young Fergie discovered that he had an accurate throwing arm. The railway tracks ran behind the house. Fergie and his friends took pleasure in throwing chunks of coal at the freight trains as they roared past. Fergie was a star when it came to hitting his target. Getting one through an open freight car door or between the speeding cars was just like getting a homerun for the young lad. Superior Tool and Dye was on the other side of the tracks, however, and sometimes its windows suffered from a direct hit. When chunks of coal were found inside the building along with the broken glass, it wasn't difficult to figure out what had happened.

Fergie also honed his pitching skill at Terry's Coal Yard where there was an ice chute with a small opening at the top - a tempting target. Even at the age of five, he could hit it dead on. The folks at Terry's began to complain to the neighbourhood that, for some strange reason, they were finding rocks embedded in their blocks of ice. Eventually they caught on, and Pops Jenkins was approached to get his son to stop aiming for the ice shute.

Dennis Steele recalls that as a teenager, Fergie used to position himself on the sidewalk in front of a vacant lot in Chatham and aim small stones across the lot, over the creek and across the railway tracks. By timing his throws carefully, he was often able to place the stone neatly between two boxcars, from a distance of about 200 feet. But from Fergie's point of view, aiming for the open door of a boxcar was more fun.

Young Ferguson's first real exposure to sports came when he was four years old. His father bought him a pair of ice skates, and he immediately liked the feel of the ice below those blades. He played on his first hockey team when he was seven, and throughout his life has continued to play at a recreational level. Like many young Canadian boys, he liked hockey a lot, and took it for granted that if he had a career in sports, it would be on the ice.

Later, the family moved to 213 Adelaide Street South which was in a mostly white area of Chatham. The house was very close to Stirling Park where Fergie and his friends often played pickup games of ball. It was here, too, that Ferguson Sr. often took his son to hit a few flies. Stirling Park became an important part of Fergie's youth.

This park which played a pivotal role in Fergie's future was named in honour of A.E. (Archie) Stirling who owned a variety store in the neighbourhood. Stirling was an avid baseball fan, and had many contacts with the Detroit Tigers and other major league

213 Adelaide Street - Home of the Jenkins family and the Adelaide Street Gang

teams. The walls of his store were covered with baseball photos and memorabilia. He was a strong supporter of local minor league baseball, and always encouraged the boys in the neighbourhood to get involved in the game.

When the family moved to this neighbourhood, Fergie began classes at Queen Mary School. He liked school, although he never excelled as a student. Nevertheless, he loved to read, especially boys' adventure tales such as Tom Sawyer, and animal stories like

Stirling Park in Chatham where Fergie Jenkins had his first exposure to sports.

Black Beauty and The Yearling. Another favourite subject was art, where he enjoyed drawing, especially scenes depicting people. His mother often remarked that she never had a problem getting Fergie off to school, and he never played hookey.

Fergie's music teacher quickly recognized his excellent singing voice. Before long he was in the school choir, and sang solos in competition in the Kiwanis Music Festivals held annually in the local schools. Fergie sang in church choirs, too, until his voice broke at the age of 15.

It was at Queen Mary School that the principal, Murray Merritt, could see a latent talent and encouraged Fergie to get involved in sports. He introduced him to volleyball, soccer, softball, and track and field events, and encouraged him to play them all.

When Fergie was eleven, he played soccer at school with a team. On one occasion, the ball went over a high wire fence and lodged in the branches of a tree. Fully confident of his tree-climbing ability, Fergie offered to go after it. He succeeded in scaling the fence, getting across to the tree, and knocking the ball back onto the field. At the same time, he lost his balance and fell headfirst from the tree. It was a natural reaction to put his hands out to break the fall. The result was a broken left wrist, a hairline fracture of the arm, and a sprained right wrist. He was rushed off to the hospital where, in spite of the pain, he smiled when introduced to the attending physician, Dr. Jenkin. The result was six weeks with casts on both arms. Fergie did not like the period of inactivity caused by the escapade.

Later, Fergie attended John McGregor Secondary School for Grades Nine and Ten. It was a long walk from Adelaide Street, especially in winter. Pops Jenkins often took pity on the boys in the neighbourhood. Whenever his schedule permitted, in bad weather he would pile the boys into his vehicle and drive them to school.

Gord Quigley, the principal at John McGregor, became another of the major influences in Fergie's young life. He, too, encouraged the young athlete to take part in a wide variety of athletic activities, even including square dancing. Fergie's sports education was surely one of the most eclectic on record.

Throughout elementary and high school, Fergie participated in almost all sports programs offered. Because of his size and natural ability, he excelled in all of them. Track and field, golf, baseball, basketball, soccer, hockey all seemed to come to him with ease. He succeeded at every new challenge. After a try at football, he gave it up, disgusted that the coaches encouraged players to be rougher than necessary. Although he was large in body, even as a teenager, he never sought to use his body for violence or bullying.

After Grade Ten, Fergie went to Chatham Vocational High where students were expected to concentrate on their studies, and were allowed to play only three sports. Fergie's choices were track, hockey and basketball. For the latter sport, he was named most valuable player three seasons in a row, and was chosen the school's Athlete of the Year for 1961-62. If he could have, he would have played baseball as well, but at that time, baseball was not part of the extra curricular activities in Ontario high schools. Throughout his high school years, Fergie won five letters for sports.

Even the local recreation centre pools were not alien territory for Fergie. He began swimming at the age of five, and his first sports competition was in a relay at the pool at Stirling Park. He continued to swim, and later earned the Royal Lifesaving Award of Merit, an advanced swimming award.

There was another sport Fergie has enjoyed for many years. At 14, he began hunting with a .22 rifle, and later he raised and trained hunting dogs on his farm. An avid fisherman as well, Fergie Jenkins can truly be called an all-around sportsman.

Of all the team sports, Fergie liked hockey best. His hockey hero was Doug Harvey, and he dreamed of becoming a defenseman. For a time, it seemed that his athletic career would be on the ice. Fergie went through all the usual levels of hockey competition - midgets, juveniles, bantams and junior - playing on the all-star teams, as well as on teams sponsored by the Jaycees and the Rotary Club of Chatham. This could have been the jumping-off point for a professional hockey career, but somehow his motivation lost momentum.

After he had 14 stitches in his forehead, plus other lacerations on his lip and eyebrow, his mother decided that the sport was just too violent. Those were the days when helmets were not required on the ice, and injuries were even more frequent and more serious than they are today.

"You're going to get banged up so I won't know you," she said. And that was that.

Fergie's second sports choice was basketball. He first hit the sports page headlines in Chatham when he was playing for the John McGregor team and scored 45 points against Ridgetown District High School. His performance was so outstanding that at the age of 16, he was invited to join the Cagers, a senior basketball team. That put him into competition with men in their 20s, and he made a good showing, consistently scoring 15 to 20 points a game.

Because of his love of basketball, Fergie hoped that he would keep growing. However, when it became obvious that his maximum height was going to be 6'5", he realized that he was not destined to be a professional hoopster. Although he did have a lot of fun with the sport along the way, playing with the Harlem Globe Trotters in the off-season from 1967 to 1969.

As for baseball, it came third on Fergie's mental list of favourite sports.

Fergie's love of sports came naturally. Both parents were involved in sports. In spite of her blindness, Delores Jenkins took up five-pin bowling, and soon had a 215 average. For four years, she was top blind woman bowler in southwestern Ontario. In fact, Delores became recreation director for the Canadian Council for the Blind in Southwestern Ontario. She was president of the local organization three times, and was elected to the executive of the Ontario Division for two terms.

Ferguson Sr. had an even greater influence on his son's feel for sport. His father, Fergie Jr.'s grandfather, had played baseball. So did the middle Ferguson. He played semi-pro baseball as an outfielder in the northern USA before moving to Chatham to play with the Black Panthers, an all-black team. Semi-pro meant that the players were paid $35 a week. Sometimes, to avoid the colour bar in the U.S., they had to say they were Indians, Ferguson Sr. recounted in later years. From 1935 to 1937, Fergie Sr. played outfield for the Chatham Coloured All-Stars, a well-known barnstorming black team made up of men from the Chatham area. Among Fergie Sr.'s special friends on the team was Earl "Flat" Chase, a player who would have made the major leagues if it hadn't been for the colour of his skin. Chase was a pitcher and first baseman.

Don Tavron, one of two surviving members of the Chatham All-Stars, recalls that Flat Chase was an outstanding player who should have been a "shoe-in" for the major leagues. There are two stories about how Flat Chase got his name. His son, Horace, says he always thought it was because his father's hairline was shaped like a flatiron at the front. His aunt, however, told him that it was because his father was "flat at the back" and had to tie his pants to hold them up. Whatever the origin of the name, Flat Chase had a great reputation as a ball player.

"He held the record for the longest ball hit in just about every park we played in," Tavron remembers. Tavron, a shortstop, and Don Washington, a catcher, were asked to go from Detroit to Chatham to play just one game with the All-Stars. They fit in so well that they were asked to stay and remained with the Chatham team for two years.

"It was the Depression, and there was no work at home anyway," says Tavron.

In 1935, the Chatham All-Stars beat the Penetanguishine team to win the Ontario Amateur Baseball Association "B" championship pennant. Tavron and Washington roomed with Fergie Jenkins Sr. while they were in Ontario. Fergie liked to cook, and Tavron liked to eat, so they became very close friends.

The Jenkins family were friends with all of the All-Stars, for the black community in Chatham was closely knit. In fact, it may have been at a ball game that Ferguson Jenkins Sr. met his future wife, Delores Jackson. Later, the Chase and Jenkins family were connected by marriage when Fergie married Kathy Williams who was a niece of Flat Chase.

In addition to Tavron, the only other living survivor of the Chatham All-Stars is Sagasta Harding of Detroit. At 93, he, too, cherishes memories of those glorious barnstorming days in Ontario.

In 2001, the Toronto Blue Jays honoured the Coloured All-Stars by playing in replicas of the bygone team's uniforms, while their opponents at Shea Stadium, the New York Mets wore the uniforms of the New York Cubans. The event was repeated in 2002 at the Skydome in Toronto. Busloads of fans and members of the All-Stars' families will be taken to Toronto for the occasion. It will be a fitting tribute to players of the past who excelled in their sport but have never before been given the recognition they deserve.

Fergie Sr. was rated as an A-one player, but he did not think of himself as exceptional. "I was OK," he said once, "but I wasn't great." Nevertheless, some said he would have been eligible for professional baseball, if only he hadn't been born too soon. Fergie Sr. loved baseball all his life. In later years, he even suited up to play for Chatham's Holiday Inn team against the team from the London Holiday Inn.

Early photos of baseball teams, both in Canada and the U.S.A., show white faces only. The two races seldom mixed on the ball diamond until much later. In fact, in December of 1867, the National Association of Base Ball Players in the U.S.A. voted against admission of any team "composed of one or more coloured persons." Later, when a club tried to introduce a black player, there was usually a protest from the other players and the fans. John McGraw, manager of the New York Giants, often tried to slip "coloured" players into his lineups by saying they were Cubans.

Later, Branch Rickey, owner of the Brooklyn Dodgers, had the courage to sign Jackie Robinson. Before signing Robinson, Rickey invited him to New York. They had a long conversation which started out in a friendly manner. Then Rickey began using racial epithets which shocked and horrified the young player. Although Rickey tried to provoke Robinson to hit him by using the worst words he could muster, Robinson did not respond. It was a test, to see if the young black man could keep calm, under the greatest provocation.

Robinson played for the Montreal Royals which was the Dodgers' farm club. He made such a good showing that the Big Leagues in the USA began to rethink their ban on black players. While the Montreal fans accepted Robinson immediately, fans across the border were not quick to do so. At first, he was taunted mercilessly. As time wore on, more black players began to appear on the baseball fields of America, and they were gradually accepted.

Rickey had a personal experience that emboldened him to sign Robinson. When he was a coach at an Ohio college, he had a black player who went on a road trip with the team. This young man was not allowed to eat with the other players, and the hotel at first refused to allow him accommodation. Rickey used his forceful personality on the hotel staff, and at last the player was permitted to stay - but only if he roomed with Rickey and "remained under his supervision". On one occasion, when Rickey returned to the room he found the player scrubbing at his hands. "I'm sorry, Mr. Rickey," the player said. "No matter how hard I scrub, this damn skin stays black." Rickey never told this story without choking up. Later, as owner of the Brooklyn Dodgers, he was able to take a strong stand in signing Jackie Robinson. On April 18, 1946 Robinson became the first black to play in the National League. That same year, Larry Dobie was the first black player in the American League.

Robinson broke the colour barrier to make it in the Big Leagues, but by then it was too late for Ferguson Jenkins Sr. It was not too late for his son, though. By the time Ferguson Jr. got into the major league system, there were many other black players. Playing in the major leagues was not an impossible dream for young Fergie. Once black players were accepted into the major leagues, the black leagues faded away.

Stirling Park was right behind the Jenkins home, and Ferguson Sr. often went out to play a little ball with his friends. Even as a very young lad, little Fergie loved the game, too.

"When I'd pick up my glove to go out, he'd know. He'd have to go along and sit on the bench," Ferguson Sr. recalled in later years.

As soon as little Fergie was old enough, father and son spent hours in the local park hitting flies and grounders and otherwise indulging in their love of baseball. It was at Stirling Park, too, where Fergie first played pick-up baseball with his friends, and began to discover that he had a real "feel" for the game.

Later, Fergie's mother pinpointed the time when her son began to take a serious interest in baseball. She bought him a sports magazine with a coloured photo of Philadelphia pitcher, Curt Simmons on the cover. The eight-year-old gazed at it for a long time, and said "I want a suit like that." No one really expected at the time that someday he would have one.

When his father took him to his first ballgame at Briggs Stadium in Detroit, Fergie saw Larry Dobie hit two home runs. That clinched it. He told his father "That's what I want to do." Of course, he was still a child then, and no one took the comment too seriously.

Young Fergie's first experience with organized ball was with the Chatham Minor Baseball Association, first playing right fielder in the Pee Wee league. Later, he was moved to first base because he was so tall and lanky, and had a long reach.

The Chatham Minor Baseball Association had been formed in 1946 after a bantam game in the same Stirling Park where Fergie had his first exposure to the sport. A group of manager, coaches and umpires got together and formed the association, supported by local service clubs. Baseball was very popular in Chatham and these men could see that the community and its young people could benefit from participation in this sport. Because of this enthusiasm for baseball, in the summer a full-time baseball co-ordinator came to Chatham to work with the youngsters. This enabled the association to provide daytime coaching for the lads while their volunteer coaches were at work. It was a good investment. In 1953, Fergie played on the first year bantam league team that won the Ontario Championship in the Ontario Baseball Association. Later, Fergie's success in the field of professional baseball helped to sustain the spirit of the sport in Chatham.

A man who was a big influence on Fergie during those early years was Casey Maynard, a coach with the Chatham Minor Baseball Association. Maynard first met Fergie when he moved in next door to the Jenkins family. At that time, he was coaching the Legion Bantams, ages 13 to 15. Fergie played first base on Maynard's team. "With a stride like his, on a sixty-foot diamond, he could really reach out a long way," Maynard remembers.

It was his pitching, however, that really impressed Maynard. On one occasion, when the team played a team from Detroit, Fergie was on the mound and struck out two of their players. Maynard heard one of them say to the other "Did you see that ball?" and the other replied, "No, I didn't see it at all."

At the time, Fergie was raising pigeons at home, and they would often roost on Maynard's roof. When Fergie wasn't pitching up to standard, Maynard would get his attention by threatening to have pigeon pie for supper.

Maynard remembers Fergie as an all-around ball player. "You could put him in any position on the field, and he could play it," he says. "Not only that, he could hit the ball, too. Not every good ballplayer could do that."

For eight years, when Fergie was playing for Chicago, about 30 coaches and umpires annually went down by bus from Chatham to attend one of the Cubs games. Casey Maynard recalls that women were never allowed on the bus except once, when they took Delores along. Fergie always met the bus with tickets for everyone, and on this occasion, he was surprised to find that his mother was getting off the bus. On these trips, Fergie always made sure that his hometown friends had a chance to go out onto the field, meet the other players, and receive autographed balls and other treasures to take home.

On one occasion, when Maynard attended a game with

Ferguson Sr., Fergie Jr. hit a homerun. After a while, an usher came up into the stands and handed Maynard the bat, as a gift from Fergie. It was a thoughtful thing to do for his friend and former coach. The bat is still cherished to this day. Maynard also has one of Fergie's famous "FJ31" Illinois licence plates from his days in Chicago.

2. The Adelaide Street Gang

The guiding light in Ferguson Jenkins' life was his mother, Delores. She loved children, and had expected to have a large family. However, her blindness put that hope beyond her reach. Nevertheless, her disability did not hinder her enjoyment of life, or her love of children. Fergie's friends were always welcome at the Jenkins home, and were treated there with the utmost love and gentleness. There always seemed to be an endless supply of wholesome treats - lemon pie, rhubarb pie, chicken - for the youngsters to enjoy. Delores was good company, and they all loved her.

Delores never allowed her blindness to interfere with her pursuit of Life. When asked about it at one time, she said "I never think about it. We are in this world, and we have to make the best of it. We can't all have what we like."

The "Adelaide Street Gang" made its headquarters at the Jenkins house. When Fergie's friends began dropping over for the evening of cards, Delores got a pack of Braille playing cards and started playing poker with them. At first they played for matchsticks, then for pennies. Delores was a good poker player, but some of her opponents didn't realize that when she dealt the Braille cards, she knew what everyone was getting in their hand. Of course she never took advantage of that extra knowledge, and the boys, even if they had thought of it, would have continued to enjoy the game.

Delores always recognized Fergie's friends as soon as they came into the house, often before they even spoke. The same was true when they met on the street or at a mall. It was one of the small things that endeared her to them.

Forty years later, the men who knew Delores when they were teenagers still speak of her with enthusiasm and affection. Some say she was a second mother to them, had a strong influence on their development as human beings.

When they were old enough to date, the Adelaide Street boys first took their girls friends home to meet their parents, then stopped off at the Jenkins home to introduce them to Delores and Pops.

Looking back on those days, Ken Milburn recalls that Delores was surrogate mother to all the boys in the Adelaide Street Gang. "From the age of eleven or 12 until I went to university, my weekends and the weekends of the rest of the group were spent at the Jenkins' home. There just aren't words to express the significance of Mrs. Jenkins' influence on my life. It's been a true honour to know Fergie as I know him. Like his parents, Fergie is generous and unselfish, a true humanitarian. My life has been enriched by the Jenkins family." Not many families receive such rave reviews from the neighbours.

Bryan Eaton who lived across the street remembers that the first time his mother met Fergie's mother was when she approached Delores to ask her to get Fergie to stop dunking Bryan so much in the local swimming pool. It was a cool first meeting. However, shortly after that, Bryan became ill from the heat while at the pool and had to go home. No one was home when he got there, so he went to the Jenkins' door. Delores took him in, phoned the doctor, followed his instructions and took care of Bryan until his mother came home. The families soon became good friends. To this day, Eaton still has some of his favourite recipes that he coaxed from Pops Jenkins.

Another of Fergie's childhood friends, Billy Atkinson, also lived across the street. He was about ten years younger than Fergie, but has vivid memories of the Jenkins household. Adelaide Street was a tight little community, and Atkinson remembers helping Pops Jenkins shovel snow and clean the dog pens when Fergie was away.

On one occasion, when he was five or six years old, Atkinson was walking past the Jenkins house on his way to school. Fergie scooped him up and put him in a tree on the front lawn, then sat on the porch talking to some friends. After a few minutes, Delores Jenkins came to the door and called out, "You better get that little guy out of the tree, Fergie. He has to get to school, and so do you, so get moving."

"Even though he was 6'5" to my 5'9'," says Atkinson, "Fergie never acted as though he was bigger, in size or importance."

In the 1970s, Atkinson became a professional ballplayer when

Fergie and Gene Dziadura with Fergie's childhood friend and pro ballplayer, Billy Atkinson at the Niagara Grape and Wine Festival, 1999. - photo by John Cain

he signed to pitch with the Montreal Expos. Billy and Fergie would often work out together. Fergie, being older and more experienced in playing professional baseball, would pass along advice and information that helped the younger player cope with the challenges of his own career in baseball, especially when it came to pitching.

Atkinson recalls that, in 1971 when he had just signed with Montreal, he was asked to do a favour for Fergie. Fergie was home in Chatham for a visit, but had to return to Chicago with his own car and a rental car. Would Atkinson drive the rental car back for him? So they set off, with smalltown Atkinson having no idea of where they were going or how to get there. When they reached Chicago, he tried to keep up with Fergie, but kept losing him in the traffic, only to find him again pulled over to the side two or three stoplights ahead. Atkinson was learning by the seat of his pants that Fergie can sometimes be impatient, and sometimes takes things for granted. Nevertheless, they eventually reached their destination.

One thing Atkinson always wanted to do was face Fergie on the diamond. It never happened. They never seemed to be in the same league at the same time. When Atkinson was with the Expos, Fergie was in the American League with Boston and Texas. Atkinson muses over the fact that three young men from Adelaide Street in Chatham became professional ballplayers - himself, Fergie and Doug Melvin. He wonders what was it about that environment that fostered this particular form of talent. Part of it at least may have been that steadying influence emanating from the Jenkins home.

The Adelaide Street Gang used to have sleepovers, and sleepouts in each other's back yards in summer. In winter, a rink would be flooded in Stirling Park where the boys would play hockey, then chat around a pot-bellied stove in the shack.

Practical jokes were part of the Adelaide Street Gang's fun. It was an unspoken rule that sooner or later, every member of the gang would have to get a pie in the face. Half of the fun was in not knowing when it was going to happen.

Some of their adventures as teenagers were risky, although no more so than those of other lads of the same age. They used to skinny dip in an old quarry near the Thames River, swinging out into the water from a rope tied to a tree. Although they weren't supposed to, sometimes they would jump off the railway bridge near Black Ridge and swim in the river there. If there were trees caught in the pilings under the bridge, they'd shake them loose and float downriver on them, waving as they went to everyone they saw on the banks.

Another caper was to go pigeon catching at night. The pigeons roosted under a trestle bridge, and the boys would paralyze them with the beam from a flashlight, then throw a net over them. Of course, someone then had to climb out and gather up the net and pigeons, then climb back again. The adventure became really exciting when a train passed overhead, and the pigeon gatherer had to cling to the trestle as well as hanging on to the pigeons.

The card games at the Jenkins home continued even after members of the Gang had graduated from high school and moved on to higher education or marriage. Whenever a few friends were in the neighbourhood at the same time, they gravitated to 213 Adelaide Street, and before long a card game would be in progress.

What did other parents think of this close relationship in the neighbourhood? Mostly, they were pleased that they knew where their sons were, and that whatever they were doing was neither illegal nor immoral. Everyone in the neighbourhood knew that the Jenkins parents would never permit any nonsense under their roof.

When Fergie became a local celebrity, nothing changed with the Adelaide Street Gang. He was still just one of the boys. When he came home for visits, they would do the same things they had always done together. Other residents of Chatham regarded him differently. Wherever he went, people in his hometown recognized him immediately. They wanted to shake his hand, buy him drinks, almost bow down before him. He was the first famous sports celebrity to come from Chatham. As a young man, he was flattered by all this attention. Sometimes his mentor, Gene Dziadura, had to give him a few words of advice.

On one occasion, Fergie was showing off by juggling a heavy glass ashtray and doing tricks with it. A slight miscue and the ashtray shattered, badly cutting his right index finger.

"Way to go, Fergie," Gene chided. "That's just what a right-handed pitcher needs - three stitches in his index finger." Fergie took the scolding without rancour, and learned another valuable lesson. Gene took his job as Fergie's coach and trainer seriously, and extended it far beyond his protégé's mere physical development. He was interested, too, in seeing Fergie become a successful human being. The two became close friends, a bond that still exists.

The Adelaide Street Gang at 213 Adelaide Street. From left to right: Len Milburn, Fergie's cousin Janet Gields, Ken Milburn, Delores Jenkins, Fergie Sr., Bill Sault, Bryan Eaton, Fergie Jr., John DeJong. - photo courtesy Brian Eaton

3. Turning Point

Fergie's chance to make an impact as a pitcher came in the Bantam league. One weekend, at a game in Kitchener, the regular pitcher Jack Howe had a sore arm. The other pitcher, Mac Cundle, had already pitched one game that weekend, so Coach Doug Allin called a team meeting and asked for a volunteer. Remembering his accuracy with the freight cars and the ice chute, and encouraged by the fact that he was already pitching in the house league, Fergie said he'd give it a try.

Although he didn't know it, it was the most important decision of his career, one that would shape his entire future. Fergie went all seven innings, allowing just two hits and striking out 15 men. His coaches knew right then that this pitcher had an extraordinary talent. They were not wrong in their assessment. Before long, professional scouts from the Tigers, the Red Sox, the Pirates, the White Sox and the Indians heard about Fergie and were giving him serious consideration.

At this point, Gene Dziadura took on an important role in Fergie's career. Dziadura had been a professional ball player as a short stop in the Chicago Cubs minor league system. He had a promising career, but in 1959 during a game in Lafayette, Louisiana, he was hit in the head by a ball. The impact dislocated a spinal disc, doing permanent damage. It was clear that Dziadura could no longer continue as a professional ballplayer. A native of Windsor, Ontario, he had a Bachelor of Arts degree from the University of Windsor. Teaching seemed to be a viable alternative to baseball, so he approached the Chatham Board of Education about a job. He later became a very popular history teacher at Chatham Collegiate Institute.

Gene Dziadura was not out of baseball completely, however. His experience and love of the sport made him a valuable asset to baseball. During the summers, he was a scout for the Philadelphia Phillies in southwestern Ontario.

In May of 1959, one of Fergie's teachers, Gerry McCaffrey, got in touch with Dziadura. He wanted Dziadura to do some substitute teaching for him while he took time off to get married. At the same time, he tipped him off about a couple of promising young players. So in May, 1959, Dziadura drove up from Windsor to have a look. He arranged to meet Jenkins and the other player at Turner Park where he put the youngsters through a gruelling workout. As Dziadura watched him work out on the baseball field, he realized that although Fergie's performance was not outstanding, it definitely showed potential for future stardom. There were some rough edges, but nothing that couldn't be corrected with a little work.

"He was a string bean," Dziadura recalls, "but he had a very flexible body. I liked the way he was loose. When he picked up the ball, it seemed very natural. He could throw the ball well, he could swing the bat nicely, and he could run with that long gait of his." Dziadura drew the lad to the attention of Tony Lucadello, one of the chief scouts for the Phillies, who, with the help of Casey Lopata arranged for a tryout camp in Chatham. Of course Gene Dziadura made sure that Fergie was there. At 15, Fergie was 6'3, weighed 155 lbs, and wore a size 12 shoe. Not only that, but he had a long reach. His right arm was destined to grow to 38½" in length, a very long reach even for a tall man.

Right from the start, it was obvious that Fergie was a natural athlete with plenty of potential. His record on the ice rink, the basketball court and elsewhere in local sports was all the evidence needed. When Dziadura spoke to coaches who had worked with Fergie previously, they all told him that the young lad was very coachable. He listened to what he was told, and followed instructions carefully. This willingness to learn was one of the keys to his success later in life. Real talent can be hampered by arrogance.

What impressed Dziadura most was the fact that when Fergie threw the ball, it flowed from his fingers like water pouring out of a glass. It was a rare gift, something he had seldom seen in a young pitcher. Gene was given the go-ahead to work with Fergie, and he did so with dedication. For three years, Gene worked on improving Fergie's pitching technique by teaching him the mechanics of throwing a baseball.

Learning how to control the ball is one of the most important lessons a pitcher learns. To develop Fergie's pinpoint accuracy, Gene rigged up a system of strings with a rectangle in the middle. Instead of squatting, a position that strained his back, he sat on a wastebasket behind the rectangle, mitt in hand to catch Fergie's pitches. As training progressed, he gradually lowered the height of the square to pitching level, then he reduced the size of the rectangle until Fergie could put the ball through it consistently. Then the size was reduced again. It was an exercise that paid off in years to come. At his peak, Jenkins could throw the ball at 90 miles an hour; even in later years, it was only a fraction slower. He could throw curves and sliders, any type of ball at all. One sports writer referred to his "William Tell accuracy". It began with that hole at the top of the ice plant chute, and developed with hours of gruelling practice with the rectangle of strings.

During one of the pitching practice sessions Gene, sitting on the wastebasket, urged Fergie to concentrate on throwing with the greatest speed possible. When Gene put out his mitt to catch the ball, it became entangled with the strings. The ball hit the wastebasket millimetres below Dziadura's crotch. The wastebasket exploded from beneath Gene and flew into the corner of the gym. As a first nervous reaction, both men laughed a little. Then Gene pointed to the dent in the wastebasket where the ball had hit. Fergie started to shake. Gene said "My God, Fergie, you're turning white!"

"Ya, Gene," Fergie replied, "but if it had hit you, you would have been black!"

The story has gone down in baseball history. Fergie told it again when he surprised Gene by turning up at his retirement party. When he got up to speak, he pointed out Gene, his children and his grandchildren.

"You know," Fergie said "if I hadn't been so accurate, you wouldn't be seeing any of these people here!"

Sometimes in their practice sessions, Dziadura and Fergie were joined by Ed Myers, another up-and-coming Chatham pitcher who was eventually signed by the Phillies and spent three years in their system. Myers reached the AA level with the Chattanooga Lookouts before an elbow injury ended his professional baseball career. He later became a teacher at Chatham Collegiate Institute and is presently teaching at Chatham-Kent Secondary School.

No matter what position he plays, it is important for a ballplayer to be a good hitter. So Fergie worked on his hitting as well. That was another exercise that paid off later on.

"I always prided myself on being able to bat," says Fergie. Pitchers weren't often noted for being excellent batters, so it was pride well earned. During his career, Fergie had 19 homeruns to his credit - not at all a bad record for a pitcher.

This intensive training was essential because U.S. high school baseball teams were often able to play year around, while the Canadian season was much shorter. To be able to match the skill and conditioning of the U.S. players he'd be coming up against in the professional world, Fergie had to have total dedication to his training program.

"Fergie was very coachable," said Gene Dziadura. "He listened to what I told him. And he was dedicated. He never missed a workout, even if it meant he had to miss a date or some other event."

From time to time, Lucadello would visit Chatham to see how things were going. One thing that Fergie did need to develop was upper body strength. When Dziadura and Lucadello realized how much Fergie loved the out-of-doors, they regularly sent him out to chop wood. Dziadura got a lot of wood stumps and put them into the backyard at 213 Adelaide Street. Then he had Fergie hold the axe with his left hand on the bottom and his righthand at the top, then let his hand slide down the handle to simulate a pitching motion. He would then raise the axe, and bring it down with a snap of his wrist, simulating the motion of throwing a ball.

"We didn't have a fireplace," Fergie remembers, "but I chopped a lot of wood." Family friends contributed the logs, bringing them to 213 Adelaide Street where Fergie obediently chopped them into kindling. As the woodpile grew, so did his shoulder, forearm, and wrist strength. In those days, there was no sophisticated weight or exercise equipment. Fergie had to rely on old-fashioned hard work, but it did the trick.

At Dziadura's recommendation, Fergie did light weight training as well. To a pitcher, strength is as important as speed and accuracy, but Dziadura didn't want Fergie to develop the bulging muscles that come from heavy weight training. Ferguson Sr. obtained a small three-pound hand sledgehammer as an exercise aid. Fergie used to sit on the couch watching television and, using a snap of his wrist, drop the sledgehammer into a pillow - over and over again - until his mother said "I wish you'd go out onto the back porch to do that!" However, the motion strengthened his wrist, developed good rotation for the release of the curve ball, and made it natural for the ball to drop from his fingers.

Around 1960, Fergie made himself a couple of weights, one ten-pound and one 25-pound. He used them faithfully to keep his muscles sound. The weights went along wherever Fergie went. For years, they were a standard part of packing for any trip, and were always handy in whatever hotel room or apartment he was occupying.

Also as part of his training, Fergie did a lot of running with Gene Dziadura. Their favourite spot was at the local golf course where they would run from tee to green. They even ran on the coldest winter days, leaving the car idling in the parking lot so that it would be warm when they got back. Running in the snow was best of all, because it was harder on the legs. On one winter day, Gene forgot a sandtrap and fell into snow up to his waist, much to Fergie's amusement.

"Fergie always loves a good joke," Gene recalls. "He has a good funny bone. He could always laugh at himself, too."

These regular practice sessions continued right up until Jenkins' retirement.

Later, when Fergie was pitching for the Chicago Cubs, he was invited to visit the Nikola Tesla School in Chicago as part of the Model Cities Program. He was asked to throw a ball with all his might at one of the new unbreakable windows being installed in some local schools at that time. In spite of the 90-mile-an-hour impact, the window held, and presumably the manufacturer got the $400,000 contract for installing their product in other Chicago schools.

Over the years, Gene Dziadura became a close friend not only of Fergie, but his whole family. They trusted his advice about the direction their sons' career should take. There were many serious conversations about the options open to Fergie, and also many purely social get-togethers such as good friends enjoy.

When Fergie was 17, Gene thought he should be playing for a Senior local team, rather than in the Juniors. After all, by that time he was almost his full 6'5" height, and as strong as many of the men. Pitching against Juniors who were smaller and weaker than he was not much of a challenge any more. Most of the Senior players were happy to have Fergie on the team, but few people criticized Gene for getting his protégé onto a team with older men. They felt it was a case of favouritism.

Fergie didn't do well in his first year with the team. He wasn't accustomed to pitching to men of equal or greater size and strength. It took a while for him to discover how to use his ability on the team. His critics felt vindicated. However, the following year, when Fergie was 18, he did much better. After one game which he was unable to attend, Dziadura asked the first baseman from Michigan how "the kid" had pitched. The reply was "Awesome!"

When Fergie graduated from high school in June, 1962, Tony Lucadello was standing by with contract and pen in hand. In those days, players were free agents, and several other teams were interested in signing Fergie. Over the years, Lucadello had developed a genuine friendship with the Jenkins family whom he had met back at that tryout camp. They had often visited and dined together, so that the relationship that began as a business connection had gone far beyond that. When the time came for signing, Fergie's parents were determined that he should sign with the Phillies and no one else. They didn't want him to negotiate with other agents, regardless of what attractive monetary rewards might be promised. They knew that Lucadello had had confidence in Fergie from the start, and had devoted three years to making sure that he was ready for the next step in his sports career. Loyalty and friendship came before money with the Jenkins.

The actual signing came shortly after Fergie graduated from high school. His father prepared a special dinner served by candlelight at 213 Adelaide Street. The group enjoyed the leisurely meal and talked about Fergie's future. At midnight, the contract and the pen were put on the table, and Fergie signed on the dotted line.

His signing bonus was $8,000, his monthly salary less than $400. His bi-weekly cheque with deductions, was $161. While that doesn't sound like much by the standards of the 21st century, it was a heady time for a 18 year-old who up until then had not even had time to hold a summer job. Instead of buying himself a flashy new car, as most young men would have done, Fergie gave the money to his parents to pay off the mortgage on their modest home.

In spite of raises in the future and many honours earned on the baseball diamond, Fergie Jenkins never earned the sort of multi-million dollar salary that to-day's professional players enjoy. Nor did advertisers clamour to have him appear in their television commercials - a substantial source of income for many athletes. It was a good living, but never excessive.

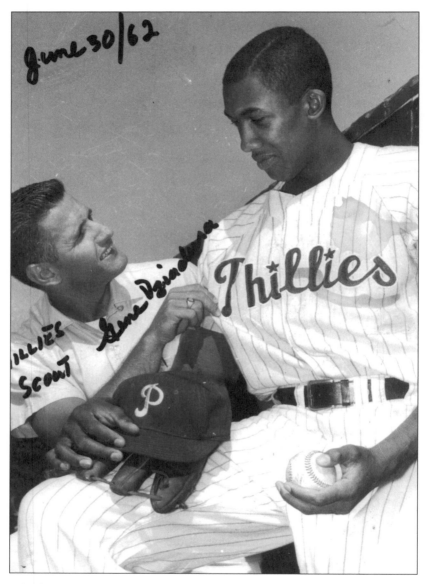

The day after Fergie's signing with the Phillies. He is wearing Gene Dziadura's Phillies uniform. - Photo courtesy Gene Dziadura

4. Off to the Minor Leagues

Almost immediately, Fergie was assigned the Phillies' Class A team in Williamsport, Pennsylvania. It was a big step in a young man's life, leaving home for the first time to enter the exciting new world of professional baseball. Gene Dziadura and Delores went with Fergie to Detroit airport. It was Fergie's first experience in a big city, a big airport. It was also to be his first trip on an airplane. As they drove closer and closer, Gene noticed that he grew quieter and quieter. Suddenly, it seemed, he was realizing that to fulfill his dream in baseball's Big Leagues, he would have to leave his familiar, small town surroundings and venture out into a huge, unknown world. It was a time of mixed elation and sadness for the young athlete.

There had been a chance that Gene might have gone to Williamsport with Fergie. Before Fergie's assignment to Williamsport, Lucadello had Gene evaluate two young infielders. After watching Gene work out with the young players, Tony asked

"How's your back doing, Gene?"

"It's not bad," Gene replied. "Why?"

Lucadello explained that the Williamsport team needed a shortstop for three weeks. Gene could be signed for that period, could fly down with Fergie and room with him. It would make the new pro feel more comfortable on his first time away from home. "But Tony!" Gene exclaimed, "I can't go. I'm getting married August 11th!" Looking back on it, Dziadura knows now that he would definitely have come back for the wedding, but if he had played well enough at this professional level and if his back seemed able to take it, he would have had a hard time pulling himself back to his jobs as high school teacher and part-time scout. He wisely said "No thanks".

So Ferguson Jenkins had to go off into his new environment all alone. When he reached Williamsport, however, the strangeness was somewhat alleviated by a ball player sent by Tony Lucadello to meet him at the airport. This was standard practice when a new rookie arrived. Every newscomer needed to feel welcome, and be put at ease.

Fergie was taken to the Williamsport Hotel where he settled into the room he was to share with Tommy Norwood. When Norwood arrived, he was shocked to discover that his roommate was black. At that time, black and white players didn't share accommodation. Weghorn promised to get it "straightened out" the next day. While not a confrontational experience, it was a foretaste for Fergie of the difference between black and white in the world of baseball. Before long, Jenkins moved into an apartment with four other black players - Richie Allen (later known as Dick), Richie Haynes, Dick Edwards and Bobby Sanders.

Tommy Norwood, like Fergie and his mentor Gene Dziadura, was one of "Tony's Boys", the name given to young players signed by Tony Lucadello. Among these were other successful players such as Grant Jackson, John Upham, Larry Cartwright, Alex Johnson and Lucadello's other Hall of Famer, Mike Schmidt.

In his first days with the team, Fergie had a lot to learn. When he was put on the mound for batting practice, he threw the ball as hard as he could. He didn't realize that the idea of batting practice was to let the batters hit the ball so that they could practice hitting the ball. The team retaliated by nailing his shoes to the floor, and tying his pants in knots. It was the usual treatment for a rookie, although Fergie didn't know that either at the time.

Shortly after, Fergie was assigned to pitch for the Miami Marlins in the Class D league. He was a little hurt at being sent there. He wondered why he couldn't stay in Williamsport and pitch for the team there. He couldn't help wondering if the club was already disenchanted with him. Nevertheless, off he went by plane to Miami.

Fergie recalls now that he was very green at the time. "I was so excited that when I got there, I didn't identify myself as a ballplayer and ask to be admitted to the park. I just bought a $2 ticket and watched the last four or five innings of the game from behind the screen. Then I went to the clubhouse and introduced myself to Andy Seminick, the old Phillies pitcher who was managing the Marlins."

Working under Andy Seminick was a good experience for Fergie at this early point in his career. Seminick had a no-nonsense approach, yet he managed to instill confidence in the young player. Although Fergie was with the Marlins for less than six weeks, that period had a lasting effect on his career.

After striking out 69 batters in 65 innings for the Marlins, he was promoted to the Buffalo Bisons to play Class AAA ball in with the International League. Once again, this was an interesting experience, transporting Fergie from a laid-back league in the south to a more upscale league where the players were older and more experienced. In the minor leagues, the players all wore casual Banlon shirts when off the field. When Fergie got to Buffalo, he discovered that the players dressed up more. "When I first went to the big leagues and saw baseball players dressed in shirts and ties and jackets, my eyes popped," he said later.

One of the advantages of the promotion was a salary increase from $400 a month to $500. This was a welcome raise, since Fergie had discovered in Florida that while $400 sounded like a lot of money to a young player, it didn't really go very far. The next spring, however, he got another raise, to $800 a month. At first, he held off signing for this amount, thinking that he was worth more. John Quinn, general manager of the Phillies, laid it on the line for him. He told him that he was doing well, but he was still inexperienced. He was being offered a substantial raise, and it was a fair offer, one that he should accept. Fergie had to admit that was true, and he signed. He was already learning a great deal.

Fergie's parents planned to attend a Bisons game in Toronto, their first opportunity to see their son in action since he turned pro. However, the game was rained out, to the entire family's disappointment.

Fergie pitching for the Marlins

5. Southern Nights

Fergie's next move in the International League was to the Little Rock Travellers. This was a deep concern for Fergie's mother. As a Canadian, her son had not suffered from the segregation and prejudice that American blacks endured. Furthermore, not so long before, Little Rock had been a very hot town when federal troops had to be sent into the city to enforce a 1954 U.S. Supreme Court ruling against segregation in public schools. Although the violence was over, there was still a strong current of negative feelings toward blacks in the South, and Dolores Jenkins was worried that they might affect her son, both on and off the field. After all, in the South, it was not unknown for a pack of white supremacists to goad a young black man into a fight so that they could beat him up.

The dynamics in the American South were very different from Chatham, Ontario where the city's 400 or so black families were accepted as part of the community. It would not be true to say that there was no discrimination at all in Chatham, but it was much more subtle than in the South. Some citizens of Chatham had no fondness for their black neighbours, and there were certain parts of the city where black people knew they were not welcome. However, there was no segregation, no separate washrooms or drinking fountains, no separate sections of the buses.

Fergie does remember that he never heard the word "nigger" until he played ball in northern Ontario during his final year of high school. Black people were seldom seen in that part of the province. But there was none of the overt violence and viciousness endured by blacks in the American South.

Fergie thought he already knew the score, of course. On one occasion when Dziadura and Fergie were driving across the border, Gene gave his protege a little advice. He put his hand on Fergie's and said "See this skin? It's white. I can make more mistakes down there [the South] than you can. If you're going to play professional baseball, you're going to run into racial discrimination. If I was playing shortstop behind you, and I made an error, people would be forgiving. But if you make mistakes like that in the South, they'll boo you because they're not so forgiving of you. That's because you're black." Fergie looked at Gene's skin, then his own, as if he had never noticed the difference before.

Gene remembered from first-hand experience that southern fans were not always forgiving, even to white players. When he played in Baton Rouge, Louisiana he found himself out on the field tossing the ball back and forth to a black player, and chatting at the same time, as he always did. Fans sitting close to him yelled at him to stop talking to a "nigger". When he later exchanged remarks with the player again, one of the fans yelled that he would get him with a knife after the game.

"At the end of the game, I can tell you I ran all the way to the clubhouse," Gene recalls. "I knew that guy was serious."

While playing in Florida, Fergie discovered that the black players had to stay in private homes rather than hotels, and he expected that the same would be true in Arkansas. Although he knew about discrimination, in his heart he really didn't believe it existed to the extent that he had been told about. He felt sure that the threat was exaggerated.

When Fergie went to the Arkansas Travellers, he and Richie Allen and Dick Quiroz were the first three black players on the team. It was a daring innovation for management, and every effort was made to make the newcomers feel welcome. Nevertheless, the men were on their guard. Fergie found himself rooming in a private home with some of the other black ballplayers. One of Fergie's roommates was Richie Allen, a friend from his Williamsport days. Allen was very nervous because he had previously had bad experiences while playing in the South. He was badly shaken when, a week or so after they arrived, he found that his car had been covered with signs bearing racial slurs. He wanted to be sent somewhere else, somewhere in the North, but the team managers persuaded him to stay. Fergie recalls that it affected Allen's entire career and attitude to Life, although he did make it to the Big Leagues.

As it turned out, a dozen or so segregationists with placards met the team at the Little Rock airport when they arrived, but on the whole Fergie and his black teammates were accepted without incident. It was the first year that the Travellers had had black players. Besides Jenkins, they were Richie Allen from Pennsylvania, Frank Barnes from Los Angeles, and Richard Quiroz and Marcellino Lopez from Cuba.

In celebration of the arrival of the first black players on their home team, about 200 blacks attended the season opener the following day. Usually, these spectators had to sit along the right field line where the view was least desirable, but on this occasion, they took seats in the grandstand without incident. It was a great show of support for the black newcomers.

Fergie did not share his mother's concerns about the South. He was simply a young man going to Little Rock to play the very best baseball he could.

"I just came to play baseball," he said in an interview. "Why would anyone want to do anything to me?" He was still a rather naïve young man from a small Canadian city.

Still, it was a shock to discover that he and his black teammates were not allowed to sleep and eat with the white players on the team. It was a new experience to find that some waitresses wouldn't serve them in a restaurant, or that hotels with "Vacancy" signs out were mysteriously full when blacks asked for a room. While white-skinned players stayed at good hotels in every city, their black teammates often were sent off to motels in the black areas of town. That was just the way it was in those days.

"It did hurt at times, though," Fergie said later. "Sometimes when the team went into a restaurant, we had to give them our money and they would bring our food out to us on the bus." Sometimes, black players were allowed to eat in the kitchen of the restaurant. Fergie preferred that to sitting on the bus, as it gave him a chance to stretch his legs and chat with the people in the kitchen.

Even this treatment didn't shake Fergie's pride in his race and his heritage. His family were good people, God-fearing churchgoers who wanted nothing more than to live their lives in the best way possible. Delores Jenkins' philosophy of life and religious dedication permeated her son's life, but she knew all too well the history of slavery and oppression that had caused her ancestors to risk their lives to reach the safety of Canadian soil.

On the whole, however, Fergie says that to this day, he has rarely experienced unpleasant racial discrimination.

Fergie's stay in Little Rock didn't last long. He didn't pitch well in his first game, against the Toronto Maple Leafs. After that, he spent his time on the bench. The team had too many pitchers anyway, and Fergie became impatient with having to sit out every game. It only took a couple of weeks for the team to decide to send him back to Class A to play with the Miami Marlins. It was a good move for all concerned, since the Marlins needed him and were prepared to give him more action. Fergie was learning that the road to the major leagues was a long one with plenty of ups and downs, even though he was just a step away from the success he dreamed of.

Fergie pitched well for the Marlins. Manager Andy Seminick liked his attitude, too. "Only 19 years old, 6'5, 205 and the best attitude you ever saw," Seminick said. "Give him a little more experience, a little better curve ball, and he'll be on his way."

Meanwhile, the folks back home weren't forgetting Fergie, and he wasn't forgetting them. He got invitations to local events such as the Annual Tyke Night held by the Chatham Junior Chamber of Commerce, the Rotary Club's Brotherhood Banquet, and Scouts' Father and Son banquets. The latter was as natural as the other invitations, for Fergie had worked his way up through Cubs and Scouts to become a Queen's Scout, one of the highest honours in Scouting.

Speaking at a Cub and Scouts banquet early in his career, Fergie told the boys that Scouting had taught him to set personal goals for himself, and to work steadily toward them. "We often don't see the results of our hard work until later in life," he told them.

In 1964, he was awarded the Sportsman of the Year Statuette presented annually by the Chatham Chamber of Commerce.

Whenever Fergie could make time in his schedule, he accepted invitations to appear in his home city and the surrounding area. He sincerely appreciated the support of local fans.

One of the most off-beat invitations Fergie had came in 1972 when he was asked to narrate The Story of Babar the Little Elephant at an afternoon concert performance by the London Symphony Orchestra. This was certainly a change of pace for the major league baseball pitcher.

All of the local newspapers followed his career closely. The *Chatham Daily News*, The *London Free Press*, and *The Windsor Star* all frequently carried stories about and photos of Fergie on their sports pages. Often there were interviews of Delores and Fergie Sr. as well. Wherever he was, Fergie made a point of calling his parents often to tell them of his latest loss or victory, and to share family news. There was a genuine love and closeness here that made these three important to each other no matter how many miles separated them. ☺

Kathy, Kelly, Fergie, Delores and Fergie Sr. - Jenkins family photo

Kelly and Fergie - Jenkins family photo

6. Latin America, Here I Come!

During the winter of 1963-64, the Phillies' protégé was sent off to play ball in Managua, Nicaragua. This was quite an adventure for a 20-year-old who had only recently left his home town. It required more than getting out onto the diamond and making a good showing there. It meant that Fergie would have to learn Spanish. That took a while.

"I like to get up early and have breakfast," Fergie relates, "but when I got to Managua, I waited until the Spanish-speaking players got up so that I could go to breakfast with them and learn how to order. Sometimes they slept in until 10 o'clock, but I waited for them. Eventually, it got easier, and I could order for myself."

By playing in Nicaragua, Fergie was able to hone his pitching skills and avoid the harsh southwestern Ontario winter at the same time. It was good experience, because many Latin American stars played there during the winter to earn money off-season and retain their skills. It was an opportunity to play against the best. Also, it was an intensive season. During the two-and-a-half to three months that he spent in Latin America between October and January, Fergie would play about 60 games. It provided a solid basis for the following season in North America.

Some North American ball players had trouble playing in the heat in Latin America. Ferguson Jenkins was never bothered by this aspect of the climate. Although from a part of the world which southerners usually think of as cold, he seemed immune to the heat. Even later, when he played in Texas and the sweltering Mid-West states, he always wore a long-sleeved undershirt under his uniform. Teammates couldn't believe their eyes when they first saw him put on a shirt in the dressing room. No matter what the outdoor temperature, Fergie suited up and played ball with astonishing consistency. The truth of the matter was that he really preferred to play in a cooler temperature, around 60° Fahrenheit, but he refused to let anything, including the weather, interfere with his concentration on the job at hand.

The habit of wearing a long-sleeved undershirt started when Gene Dziadura was training Fergie who loved to drive around with his arm on the open car window.

"Get a long-sleeved shirt on," Dziadura told Fergie. "You never know what the wind will do to that arm."

During these trips to the tropics to play winter baseball, Fergie sent home all the newspaper clippings that referred to him. Most of them were written in Spanish, so Delores would give them to Bryan Eaton who took them over to the Ursuline convent where one of the nuns translated them into English for her. Then they would be pasted carefully into a scrapbook with all the other items and memorabilia from her son's career. As time went by, the scrapbooks grew fatter, and multiplied in number.

In 1964-65, Fergie became a popular pitcher with the Cayuga team in the Puerto Rican Winter Baseball League, and was chosen to play for the League's All-Star team. By the time he returned home, he had compiled the lowest earned run average in the history of the Puerto Rican league. He also broke a ten-year record with his 1.24 runs-per-game average. With those statistics under his belt, Fergie hoped that he would be chosen as starter pitcher for the Phillies. His name was one of four in line for the job.

"I hope I get a shot as a starter," he said at the time, "but if they want me in the bullpen, I'll take it." He felt that his running had improved vastly over the winter season, and so had his control. As a parting word, the Caygua manager Frank Luccesshi said, "I don't want to see you at our Triple A camp this year. We've sent in good reports about you and there's no reason you can't stick." Fergie totally agreed.

When he returned home in January, after each winter season, Fergie would resume his training schedule with Gene Dziadura, so that there was never a time when he was allowed to get "soft" and lose his conditioning. Then when spring came, he was ready for the coming season.

7. Chatanooga Choo Choo

After his first season in Latin America, Fergie was off to the Southern Baseball AA League to play with the Chattanooga Lookouts. For the first time, Fergie's parents were able to see their son play. Along with Fergie's fiance, Kathy Williams and two of his cousins, they drove to Chattanooga to attend a game which pitted the Lookouts against the Charlotte, North Carolina team. This was a great thrill for the entire Jenkins party. It helped to make up for the disappointment Delores and Ferguson Sr. had felt when they had planned to see their son pitch in Toronto two years before, and the game was rained out.

After that, Delores loved to attend a game with her portable radio by her side. Although she couldn't see the game, she could follow the play by listening to the play-by-play commentary. She seemed to sense the tempo of the game from the crowd around her, and always knew exactly when to jump up and cheer with the crowd.

It was an additional thrill, on the Chattanooga trip, for the Jenkins family to know that the newspapers were calling Fergie "Sky High" Jenkins, not because of his height, but because he leaped sky high in the ninth to catch a bounder and put the opposing team out. The *Chattanooga News Free Press* added to the thrill by referring to Fergie as "Satchel Paige in his youth", a mighty big compliment for the 20-year-old athlete.

Fergie made a good showing with the Lookouts, hurling ten wins in a row. He was hitting well, too. This year he made the Southern League's All-Star team. Pitching scout Cal McLish was watching the young pitcher closely. Consequently, Fergie was called up to Phillies AAA Pacific Coast League farm club in Little Rock, Arkansas. He'd played for this team before, so with some trepidation, he drove from Chattanooga to Little Rock. He hoped he'd get more action than on his previous stint with the Little Rock team. As it turned out, that is exactly what happened. He was barely out of the car before he found himself in a Travellers' uniform. The next day, he was on the mound. In a double-header, he pitched to a 1-0 victory against Salt Lake City. This time in Little Rock, he was on the way to a more impressive record.

When a poll was held allowing fans to vote for the "Most Popular Traveller", Fergie won by a landslide.

Before long, there was talk that Fergie might be headed for the big leagues at last. Fans in Chatham and elsewhere were so excited by his performance and popularity that they felt the move was imminent. To quell the fervor and prevent disappointment, Phillies scout W. D. McIntyre pointed out publicly that Fergie had had only two-and-a-half years' experience in minor league baseball, while most players had four or five years in the minors before moving up.

At last, Fergie was offered a major league contract, and was told to report to the Phillies' training camp at Clearwater, Florida in February, 1965. Before he left for the two-day drive home from Little Rock to Chatham, Fergie dropped in at Little Rock Stadium to say good-bye to some of his friends. He was only gone 15 minutes, but in that length of time, thieves broke into his car and stole four suits, as well as shirts and other clothing. It was a sad way to leave a city where he had enjoyed success and adulation.

To get ready for spring training, he worked out regularly in Chatham, doing one-and-a-half hour sessions with Gene Dziadura to improve his pitching form and windup. On top of that there were daily sessions of walking, running, weight lifting and swimming. The November to January schedule with Dziadura continued every year until Fergie's retirement. It kept them both in excellent physical condition.

8. The Big Leagues at Last!

An athlete doesn't get his picture on the cover of *Macleans* magazine and on about 40 sports cards unless he has achieved more than average statistics. When Fergie finally made it to the Big Leagues, it was the fulfillment of a lifetime dream, and he was not disappointed. Nor were the fans and the club owners. But it took a little time for success to set in. Fergie learned that, in spite of talent and ambition, success does not necessarily come easily.

Fergie went first to the Philadelphia Phillies, the club that had originally signed him and sent him out into its minor leagues. It was his expectation that he would remain there for a long time. For one thing, it was going to be exciting to play in famous Connie Mack Stadium. Originally called Shibe Park in honour of Ben Shibe who was a baseball manufacturer and the principal owner of the original Philadelphia Athletics, this ball field was renamed for the Athletics' manager in 1953. There had been suggestions for years that the park should be renamed for Mack, but he consistently turned thumbs down on the idea. While he was on holiday in Florida, however, the board of directors finally took matters into their own hands and changed the name anyway. From 1953 until it was demolished in 1970, the park bore Connie Mack's name. A church now stands on the site.

Things did not go well for Fergie in Philadelphia. Spring training seemed to go smoothly, and Fergie had the impression that manager Gene Mauch was satisfied with his performance. But shortly before the start of the season, he was called into Mauch's office. With a heavy heart, he learned that Mauch was not at all satisfied. He told Jenkins that he would never win in the major leagues with "that fastball." Although he appreciated his hard work, he told him that he needed more experience, and consequently he was sending him back to Little Rock. After the euphoria of being in the Big League at last, that was bitter disappointment. The pain and hurt lingered for a while.

Neverthless, Fergie went to Little Rock intending to do his best, and he had a good season with the team there. He won eight

Fergie in the Cubs' locker room, wearing uniform #31

games, lost six, and had an earned run average of 2.95. It was a good showing, and by September Mauch had decided that he wanted him back. Fergie found himself in a Phillies uniform for the first time during a regular season.

On September 6th, he pitched in his first major league game against St. Louis. After four-and-a-third innings of solid relief pitching by Fergie, the score was 4-3 for the Phillies. Fergie was jubilant that he had won the very first major league game he pitched. He was excited enough to call home that very night. He learned that someone had called his parents to tell them that the game was being broadcast on the radio, and that Fergie was on the mound. The Jenkins quickly tuned their radio to the game, and with visitors from the neighbourhood, listened in with excitement. Even Bryan Eaton who wasn't even a baseball fan was caught up in the intensity of the occasion.

Fergie pitched in six more games before the end of the season in a total of 13 innings. He had made a decent showing with a 2-1 record, having struck out 10 and walked only two. At the end of the season, he had planned to take a rest from baseball. However, in October, he changed his mind and went off to Puerto Rico to play winter ball, confident that he would be with the Phillies for a long time. He did well in Puerto Rico, too, pitching in 40 games with an earned run average of 1.24. A good season of winter ball gave him the added confidence he needed for the season ahead with the Phillies. He had developed both his slider, and his control over the ball. He was glad he went.

During the 1966 season, the Phillies were determined to win the pennant. To do that, they needed strong pitching on the team, experienced pitchers. It looked as though they had the strength, but Fergie was new on the scene. Unfortunately, the press had not been kind to him. Media criticism definitely effected his career at this time. Reports came out during spring training that he would never succeed in the big leagues, and ought to get more experience at the AAA level. According to his critics in *Baseball Digest* and elsewhere, Fergie just didn't throw hard enough or fast enough. He didn't pay much attention to the criticism, believing that he was doing well, and had the Phillies' confidence. But when the season began, he found himself sitting in the bullpen all the time. He was bored, and began to wonder when he was going to get a chance to pitch. He hoped it would be soon.

On April 21st, 1966, he was called into Gene Mauch's office, along with Adolfo Phillips, an outfielder, and John Herrnstein who played both outfield and first base. The three were told that they had been traded to the Chicago Cubs for two tried-and-true pitchers, Bob Buhl and Larry Jackson. That was another hurt for Fergie. He had originally signed with the Phillies because he had good friends who were associated with the club, and he wanted to stay with the Phillies. It was painful to know that the head office of the Phillies did not include Fergie in their future plans. It seemed that even after all their support in the past and his hard work in the present, he was not up to their standards. Both Tony Lucadello and Gene Dziadura were upset that their protégé had been traded away. They had devoted a great deal of time to bringing him along to this point in his career, and it was a letdown to realize that their efforts were no longer going to benefit the Phillies.

Kathy was in Philadelphia with Fergie at the time. He phoned her from the ballpark and told her to start packing so they could leave for Chicago immediately. As they hastily gathered up their belongings, Kathy did her best to comfort her disappointed husband. Now that the decision had been made for them, they were eager to get out of Philadelphia and off to their new home. After driving all night, they got to Chicago on the morning of April 22nd.

When Fergie read in the newspaper a few days later that Mauch said that he was traded because he didn't throw hard enough, his hurt turned to anger. In future, he was determined to prove to the Phillies that he really did have a "big league fast ball." Every time he came up against Philadelphia after that, he made the point by giving them the full force of his pitch. In 1971, he pitched six games against them, and won them all. His overall record against the Phillies was 23 to 6.

In his post-Phillies career, he won 284 games and had six straight years as a 20-game winner. In each of the seasons from 1967 to 1971, and again in 1974 he chalked up 200 strikeouts. During his career, he struck out 3,192 batters. He was the fourth player to win 100 games in both the American League and the National League. More often than not, the letter "W" for Winning Pitcher appeared next to his name in the box scores. Not bad, for a player who was considered not quite good enough by the Phillies management.

9. Wrigley Field

When Jenkins was traded to the Chicago Cubs, one newspaper headline read "Ferguson Who?" Outfielder Adolfo Phillips went from the Phillies to the Cubs with Fergie, and for some reason he got all the attention when they arrived. Everyone expected big things from Phillips, but Fergie was almost completely ignored. Within a few months, Phillips had faded somewhat from the limelight, and Jenkins was no longer "Ferguson Who?" Baseball fans everywhere knew about the sensational young pitcher wearing the number 31 on his Cubs jersey.

Of Adolfo Phillips, Leo Durocher later said "He has the ability of Willie Mays, and he could make a fortune playing baseball, if he wanted to play baseball."

At that time, Durocher was trying to build up a younger club, in the hope of creating a team that would take the Cubs to the World Series. He didn't see Fergie's youth and inexperience as a liability. Instead, he and the Cubs scouts saw Fergie's youth as an advantage that would give him the opportunity to improve as he matured.

During the 1966 season, Jenkins started out as relief pitcher. He had six wins. Halfway through the season, it became evident that Cubs management had to make some changes. On August 25th, manager Leo Durocher said "That boy is not going to be a relief pitcher. He's going to be a starting pitcher." In Durocher's famous words, "the rest is history." Durocher had Jenkins pitch every fourth day for the next six years. It was during that period that Fergie had a sensational series of 20-win seasons.

Before long, Durocher was singing Fergie's praises. "I won't say Holtzman and Jenkins are untouchables," he said, "But if anyone wants one or the other, they're going to have to give us a bundle." Instead of sending Fergie off to play winter ball in Central America, Durocher wanted him to stay home and rest. It was a great opportunity for Fergie to spend time with his family, and to do some of the things he loves - hunt, travel a bit with

Fergie slides into home plate in a game with San Diego

Kathy, work out in the gym with Gene Dziadura.

When Fergie signed his 1967 contract, he got a deal that seemed like "a bundle" to him at the time. His salary was doubled to $20,000.

At the end of the 1966 season, Chatham celebrated Fergie's success with a two-page spread in the *Chatham Daily News*. The huge headline said "Welcome Home Fergie". Thirty-two local businesses sponsored the page with sub-headlines "Well Done Fergie" and "Way To Fire Lad".

The following year, the newspaper spread was even bigger, and Chatham Mayor Garnet Newkirk proclaimed October 21st "Fergie Jenkins Day." A Fergie Jenkins sweat shirt was designed and put on sale with the proceeds to go to a charity of Fergie's choice. In the afternoon, there was a grand parade, with Ernie Banks, first baseman for the Chicago Cubs riding with his wife in the car behind Fergie and Kathy's. In the evening, about 650 people turned out to a banquet at Kinsmen Auditorium to honour Chatham's hero and native son. Prime Minister Lester Pearson and federal Health and Welfare Minister Judy LaMarsh were invited for the occasion. Neither was able to attend, but both sent official letters of congratulation. Provincial Minister without Portfolio, Darcy McKeough presented Fergie with a scroll from Premier John Robarts. Mark Stirling was on hand to present Fergie with a gold baseball bat on behalf of his father, Archie Stirling who had played an important part in organizing the whole affair. No doubt about it. Ferguson Jenkins was and still is Chatham's greatest all-time hero. Nor has he ever forgotten Chatham. He still has the gold bat and all the other treasures presented to him that day.

On Opening Day in 1967, Fergie Sr. and Delores drove to Chicago to see the game. Delores was so excited that she couldn't sleep on the overnight trip. Fergie didn't know they were coming because they hadn't wanted to throw him off balance just before a game. But when he finished his warmup, he turned and spotted them in the stands. He went over and spoke quietly to them, took his mother's hand briefly, and shook his father's hand.

When he walked back to the dugout, Delores asked her husband, "Did he smile, Dad?"

"No, babe, he didn't," Fergie Sr. replied sadly. It wasn't the sort of warm greeting any of them wanted, nor was the time right. Yet there was a closeness in that family that made it possible for Fergie's parents to understand what had just happened. They realized that their son had been awake all night, thinking about pitching for the season opener, and trying to focus his thoughts on the job. Now he was just a little angry that his concentration had been broken. After all, winning the season opener had very high priority.

The first three innings proved that the unexpected meeting had interrupted Fergie's concentration. Then Delores jumped out of her seat and yelled "C'mon, baby! C'mon, Fergie!" He must have heard her, because he won the game. The fans were happy, Durocher was happy, and the Jenkins family was happy.

Fergie learned a lesson from that incident. In future, he invited his parents to attend the first home game of the season so there'd be no more surprises on that day.

Chatham's Mr. Baseball, Archie Stirling, was so impressed with Fergie's performance on this occasion that he sent off a telegram of congratulations. For the young graduate of Chatham's minor leagues, it was a great compliment. When the Chatham Minor Baseball Association hosted the annual Ontario Baseball Association convention, members hustled around Chatham streets putting signs on telephone poles that identified the city as "Home of Fergie Jenkins."

The year 1967 was a good one for Fergie Jenkins. In that season, he had 206 strikeouts which turned out to be a club record. The old record was set in 1909 when Orval Overall had 205 strikeouts.

In his second full season with the Chicago Cubs, Jenkins found himself on the mound facing a baseball legend. In the 1967 All-Star game Fergie pitched to none other than the famous New York Yankees' slugger, Mickey Mantle. Mantle, famous as the best switch-hitter ever, was pinch-hitting that day. Those not "in the know" often think a pinch-hitter is someone who is just filling in for someone else. That's not the case. The pinch-hitter's role is very important. He is used not only to start a rally but also, in most cases, to get a key hit to drive in a run. On this particular day, it was the fourth inning of the All-Star game with the National League ahead 1-0, two out, and the tying run on first base.

The All-Star manager, Walter Alston, walked out to the mound, expecting that he'd have to reassure the young pitcher, perhaps bolster his confidence.

"You know who the pinch hitter is?" he asked. Jenkins replied calmly that he did.

"Just throw strikes, no soft stuff" Alston said. Fergie nodded. He followed orders, and the mighty Mickey Mantle struck out. During his career, other great hitters that Fergie faced were Rod Carew, Harmon Killebrew, Tony Consigliaro and Carl Yastremski.

They all knew they had a formidible adversary in Ferguson Jenkins.

Later, Fergie was asked how he felt when he struck Mantle out. He replied "I felt like shaking hands with him TWICE - once when he got that standing ovation, and once when he let that third strike go by!"

The entire city of Chicago and the surrounding area was in a frenzy of anticipation on July 2nd, 1967. A sell-out crowd of 40,464 watched the Cubs beat the Cincinnati Reds 4-1 in a game that put the Cubs into the running for the pennant. Fan enthusiasm was so high that spectators started lining up at the gate at 8.30 a.m. Tickets were completely sold out half-an-hour before the game began. Wrigley Field was bursting at the seams. Nearly 10,000 disappointed fans were turned away, while others watched the game from apartment house roofs across the street. After the game, the fans went wild in a riotous demonstration of joy. Fergie's three-hit game earned him the greatest cheers of all.

Phil Wrigley who had been dejected by a series of losses said to a reporter "When things aren't going well, they're 'Wrigley's Cubs'. If they get a few games winning streak, they become 'our Cubs'. Can you figure it out?" Suddenly, the Cubs had been adopted with renewed enthusiasm by the people of Chicago.

For the first time in that 1967 season, Fergie won 20 games for the Cubs. It should not be forgotten that of the 15 he lost, five were 1-0 defeats - a truly enviable record for a young pitcher. Fergie laughingly referred to himself as a "daylight pitcher." At that time, the Cubs were the only major league team that did not have lights in their ball park, so all their home games were played in the afternoon.

Jenkins remembers the 1969 season with the Cubs as the year the team had an international team. There were players with ethnic backgrounds from Poland, Ukraine, Cuba, Italy, Panama, Greece, Germany and, of course, Canada. Later, he reminisced that the 1969 Cubs were one of the best teams he ever played with.

"Everyone was really nice," he says. "We all got along well

together."

While with the Cubs, Fergie achieved many "firsts". He was the first pitcher ever to win the Cy Young Award while wearing a Cubs uniform. He was the first player to win more than 100 games in a small park like Wrigley Field; he won 197 games for the Cubs at Wrigley Field. He was the all-time strikeout leader with the Cubs, getting a total of 2,038 strikeouts. He held the Cubs' record for strikeouts in one season with 274 strikeouts during 1970. His ratio of strikeouts to walks was three to one (3,192 strikeouts to 997 walks), a record that rates with such Hall of Fame greats as Sandy Koufax, Walter Johnson and Bob Gibson.

Many great pitchers are not especially good at batting or running. Nowadays, many of them go to college where they play on teams that have pinch-hitters; they don't have the opportunity or the motivation to develop these skills. Besides, in the American League at the beginning of a game, one player is often named designated hitter so that he can hit in place of the pitchers. This does not give the pitchers the incentive or need to improve their hitting and running.

In the National League, pitchers hit 9th in the batting order. Jenkins always enjoyed hitting and since he swung the bat well and was a good runner, he was called to pinch-hit on a few occasions. One year his batting average was 250, but most of the time it was 215 to 220 ("about what I weigh now," Fergie jokes) which is not outstanding. Nevertheless, during his career as a pitcher, Fergie managed to hit 19 homeruns.

One of the things Fergie did not like about being up to bat was the number of times he got hit or brushbacked. When a pitcher normally has good control, but he hits the batter or brushes the ball across his chest so that the batter has to move back, it's obvious that the pitch is deliberately aimed. Usually, it's not so much a case of personal dislike as an order from the manager who wants to see a good batter thrown off balance and lose concentration. Fergie often got hit, and sometimes was limping from several pitches that hit his legs. In a way, it was a compliment that he was good enough to be a threat to the opposing team when at bat. Nevertheless, he was never happy about the bruises, or the pain associated with them.

When on the mound, he made it a matter of personal pride never to hit a batter on purpose. He wanted to strike out a batter using his special skill, not by devious methods.

Perhaps there was some venom in those brushbacks on Fergie. To counter-balance his superb pitching, opposing teams had to start their best players against him, and use all the means at their disposal to put him off-balance. There were a lot of other good pitchers in the League at the time - Don Drysdale, Juan Marichal, Bob Gibson, Tom Seaver, for example - and when it was Fergie's turn to pitch, he always had to start against the best. Although Fergie was known as "the ultimate control pitcher", there was a lot of pressure on him to win against these diamond stars. Fortunately, this sort of pressure didn't seem to bother Fergie. He had learned to focus on the job at hand, and shut out everything else while he was on the mound. In the end, he was the only major league pitcher in history to strike out more than 3,000 hitters, at the same time allowing less than 1,000 walks. Learning to concentrate totally had really paid off.

When asked in later years if there was ever a batter he was afraid of, Fergie thought carefully, then said, "There was one guy. Willie McCovey, first baseman with the [San Francisco] Giants. He was about 240 lbs., 6'6", and he could really hit. He hit alot straight down the centre, and if you got in the way of one of them, it was pretty bad. "After all, the pitcher is pretty close to the batter at that point".

It was during this period in Chicago when Jenkins noticed the licence plate on Ernie Banks' car. It was "EB14" - his initials plus his uniform number. Fergie went down to the licence bureau and applied for "FJ31". It took 15 working days to get it, but he was mighty pleased when it arrived. He continued to use this licence plate for ten years. When plates had to be replaced each year at renewal time, he kept the old ones and still has them "somewhere around."

Fergie stops to help an injured Cub, Jose Cardinal who was trying to steal home plate at Wrigley field

10. Chew, Chew, Chew That Bubble Gum

At the end of the 20th century, ball players were criticized harshly for chewing tobacco and making a show of spitting in front of fans and television cameras. Ironically, the baseball card industry began back in the mid-1880s when tobacco cigarette smoking was coming into vogue. With the invention of a machine that produced ready-made cigarettes, the finished product was marketed in paper packages. Soon it was discovered that many packages were crushed, so a card was inserted to stiffen the pack. As an added attraction, the cards were printed with pictures of actors, actresses and baseball players. By then, baseball was becoming a popular spectator sport, and the connection with sports celebrities helped to get rid of the idea prevalent at that time that ready-made cigarettes were effeminate. Real men still rolled their own.

As time went by, there was no need to promote cigarettes - it was popular enough without the extra advertising. So the idea of baseball cards was taken up by other industries. When Fleer Corporation invented bubble gum in 1928, a new market was created for sports cards. Bubble gum and sports cards became synonymous with the game of baseball.

Early in his baseball career, Fergie Jenkins tried chewing tobacco like his fellow players, but he soon discovered that he disliked it. Besides, the juice ran down his throat, and caused some infection in his back teeth, which in turn caused some pain in his pitching shoulder and arm. He turned instead to Wrigley's Doublemint gum. When he was signed by the Philadelphia Phillies, like the other players there, he switched to bubble gum. Many major league players signed contracts with bubble gum companies to allow their photos to appear on bubble gum cards. In return for a five-year contract, they received $250 plus a gift of some sort - a television set, a VCR, a washing machine - and a case of bubble gum. All the players chewed, and some blew better bubbles than others. The clubs encouraged it, even supplying bubble gum in a selection of flavours such as sour apple, sour peach, strident etc. After all, it was a harmless habit, compared to the risks of chewing tobacco.

When he was signed by the Chicago Cubs, however, Fergie got a tongue lashing from manager Leo "The Lip" Durocher for chewing bubble gum. It seems that a television camera had caught Fergie on the mound blowing a bubble "as big as a grapefruit." Far from being praised for his skill in this regard, Fergie was blasted. Why? The president of the Cubs, Philip K. Wrigley (after whom the Cubs' home park Wrigley Field was named, incidentally) was also president of the world's largest chewing gum company, and it didn't make bubble gum!

Down in the locker room, Durocher gave the team a lecture about bubble gum. "At no time...never, never, never...will any of you chew bubble gum again!" Then Durocher turned to Fergie and yelled, "If I catch you chewing bubble gum again, I'll send you so far down into the minors that a 10-cent stamp won't reach you!"

"Yes, sir," Fergie replied meekly. He was really scared. He was still new to the team, and Durocher could be intimidating. Like many other major league players, Fergie liked to have something in his mouth when in the bullpen or out on the field. Gum was an acceptable alternative to tobacco or the toothpick that some other players favoured. After that reaming out from Durocher, Fergie switched back to Wrigley's Doublemint gum, always carrying a few packages into the dugout, then flashing them so that the television cameras would pick up the nationally-known yellow wrapper.

In spite of this, Fergie appeared on 40 baseball cards. His rookie card is now worth about $400. Casey Maynard took his grandson to a mall in Detroit one day, and there they found one of Fergie's baseball cards on sale. The price was $5. When Maynard told the vendor that he had coached Fergie as a youngster, the price went down to $1, so the card became the prized possession of the grandson. Maynard later asked Fergie to autograph it, but Fergie declined saying, "No, I won't do that. It's worth more to you unsigned."

Fergie was right. Once a card has been signed, it is no longer considered to be in mint condition. The value is then in the autograph alone, and because a vast number of sports autographs are forgeries, many dealers don't want to have anything to do with them.

From left to right: Brent Lawler, John Oddi, Carl Kovacs, John Pelizzari, Bill Berg, Fergie Jenkins, and Bert Campameris

Carl Kovacs, Gary Thomson, Fergie Jenkins, John Oddi and John Outlaw at Camp Maple Leaf.

11. Leo The Lip

Throughout the baseball world, Leo Durocher was known as a great ball player, a great manager and an abrasive, sometimes abusive person. Durocher is still quoted frequently, for he originated the saying "Nice guys finish last." This saying, incidentally, is almost always quoted incorrectly. On July 6th, 1946, as Durocher's players walked up the steps, he said "Walker, Cooper, Mize, Marshall, Kerr, Gordon, Thomson . Take a look at them. All nice guys. They'll finish last. Nice guys. Finish last." He lived up to his own standard of success. He later said "I came here to win, not to lose."

Durocher was a man to be admired in many ways. He'd played professionally with the New York Yankees, the Cincinnati Reds, the St. Louis Cardinals, and the Brooklyn Dodgers before becoming a manager. Under him, the Dodgers won their first National League championship in 21 years, and the New York Giants won the National League pennant in 1951 and 1954 before going on to win the World Series in 1954. From 1961 to 1964, Durocher coached the Los Angeles Dodgers, then he moved on to the Chicago Cubs. He and Jenkins came on board with the Chicago Cubs at about the same time.

Ferguson Jenkins sometimes has referred to him this way. "When I was seven or eight years old, I got introduced to Christ through the Church. When I was fourteen years old, I was baptized. And when I was 23, I finally met the devil. His name is Leo Durocher."

But the first time Fergie met Durocher, he didn't feel that way. It was on Friday, April 22nd, 1966 - Jenkins' first day with the Chicago Cubs. He'd driven all night to get to Chicago, and had just arrived in town with Kathy. He immediately headed out to Wrigley Field. He'd no sooner introduced himself to the other players and some of the staff than he found himself wearing a Cubs uniform with 31 on the back. In Philadelphia, his number had been 30, but that one was already in use on the Chicago team, so he took what was available. Within a few minutes of his arrival, he found himself out on the field shagging balls. Suddenly he heard a harsh voice yelling,

"Hey, number 31, come over here. I want to talk to you." It was Leo Durocher. The two men shook hands and spoke briefly about Fergie's recent pitching history. Then they parted. Fergie wasn't overly impressed with Durocher, and really knew nothing about him. All he saw was a short, bald, elderly man with a voice like "shark's teeth" and an abrupt manner. He rather liked the guy. They were soon to become much better acquainted.

The following day, April 23rd, Fergie pitched for the Cubs for the first time. It was a memorable occasion for him. The Cubs were playing the Dodgers, and the Cubs were last place in the league. By the third inning, the Cubs were struggling, and Durocher decided he needed a right-handed pitcher. Fergie was in the bullpen warming up at the time, and he was chosen to go out onto the mound. It was a hard-fought game, but the Cubs won 2-0.

The *Chicago Sun-Times* sportswriter stated in no uncertain terms that on that day, a star had been born at Wrigley Field - Ferguson Arthur Jenkins. It was a great thrill for the young pitcher who had recently suffered so many rebuffs and setbacks in the baseball world.

At first, Durocher seemed to stand up for Jenkins. For example, shortly after Fergie was chosen for the All-Star team, the Cubs were in Pittsburgh. Before a game against the Pirates, Fergie went into the batting cage for some practice. The pitcher was Dean Burk. He threw a ball directly at Fergie and hit him in the back. All the players who were watching started yelling and laughing. Fergie was so angry that he stepped out of the cage, and only went back when Al Spangler replaced Burk on the mound. This time, Spangler threw a ball that hit him on the leg. Once again, there was a lot of jeering. Fergie stomped off to the locker room, took off his uniform and stepped into the shower. When Durocher heard about it, he let the players have it. For the next few days, he made frequent visits to the batting cage, just to make sure there were no more similar incidents.

When you were in Durocher's good books, everything went well. Leo loved to play cards, and had games going all day long with his favourites. One of the features of these games was that the players hurled a steady stream of insults at each other as the cards hit the table, but they were friendly insults. Sometimes they'd be card buddies for months, then something would upset Leo. His blue eyes would turn cold, and he'd totally ignore the player who had earned his disdain.

Throughout the 1966 season, Jenkins was relief pitcher in 51 games. Then in July, Durocher came to him and said "We're short of starting pitchers. I'm going to start you against New York on Saturday."

Fergie was happy pitching relief, and said so. But Durocher insisted, and Fergie became a starting pitcher. His comment that he was happy to stay in the bullpen was picked up by the press and interpreted to mean that he wasn't anxious to be a starter. It was a case of the press reading more into the remark than was intended. Fergie was as pleased as any pitcher would be to be chosen. He was just letting Durocher know that he was not dissatisfied with things as they were.

Later, when Durocher was asked if he had done anything to change Jenkins after he came to the Cubs, he replied "Yes, I changed him from a reliever to a starter."

As it turned out, that first good game proved to Durocher that he had made the right choice. Fergie pitched eight innings, with the score tied at 3-3. Durocher was delighted.

"We've found another starting pitcher," he declared. "Fergie's beautiful. He's not afraid to challenge the hitters."

A month later, Jenkins pitched 8½ innings against the Atlanta Braves, clinching Durocher's enthusiasm for his pitching skills. The Cubs did well that season. Fergie felt that that season was the turning point in his career. He and Kathy found an apartment on the South Side of Chicago, and began to make friends. That season, Fergie made $8,000. At the end of the season, he spent some time in Scottsdale at the Cubs' rookie school. Fergie was not exactly pleased to be sent off to rookie school, but the training seemed worthwhile. He made such good progress that his time there was cut from three weeks to two.

Then he and Kathy went home to stay with their families for a while. While there, Fergie got a temporary job selling cars for Rossini Brothers in Chatham. He did a lot of personal appearances at local events, too. One of his favourites was being asked to drop the puck at an OHA Junior B hockey game in Blenheim near Chatham.

At one time, during the off-season, he also modelled suits and shoes for O'Connor & Goldberg "Where Chicago's Finest Athletes Buy Chicago's Finest Footwear". This was one of his few opportunities to venture into the field of advertising. Generally speaking,

Looking good - Fergie models suits for a Montreal company

Fergie always has been a conservative dresser, but he is fond of stylish clothes. During his years with the Cubs, he changed to the mod style and let his hair grow a little longer. He chose suits with the Nehru collar for dress occasions, and turtleneck shirts and beads for more casual times.

On one occasion, two radio sportscasters commented on the outfit Fergie was wearing when he arrived at the ballpark. They were impressed by his long-sleeved white turtleneck sweater, white pants, white socks, white shoes and double-breasted blue sports jacket with white stripes.

"Man, it was something to see," one of them exclaimed.

In the spring, Durocher made it clear to Fergie that he would have to work hard to maintain his position as a starter. Fergie buckled down, and all the hard work bore fruit. The team did well. Durocher's baseball strategies were legendary, and were making progress in developing a strong team. The fans responded accordingly, giving their home team enthusiastic support. Jenkins won eight of his first 11 games, and was chosen as one of the pitchers for the National League All-Star team.

At the end of September, 1967, Fergie pitched his 20th winning game of the season. He received telegrams of congratulations from Premier John Robarts, and the Hon. Darcy McKeough, Minister Without Portfolio for Ontario, proof that his home province's pride went all the way to the top.

Fergie was by no means Durocher's favourite. He earned the managers' ire in March, 1968 during spring training in Scottsdale. When Fergie and some friends went horseback riding, Fergie's horse suddenly spooked, and ran out of control into another horse, then threw its rider into a framed metal fence. Fergie was badly bruised, including a bad bruise on his right hip. When he called Durocher to tell him the news, "The Lip" was furious. He immediately scratched Fergie as starting pitcher in the Cubs' the season opener in Cincinnati. But the following night, Fergie was scheduled to play, so he used plenty of ice on his injured hip and loaded up on painkillers. Later, he couldn't remember being out on the mound, but the Cubs won 10-3, and he struck out twelve men.

Durocher had a point regarding Fergie's injury, and possible injuries in team basketball games. There was a ruling usually called the Lonborg Law after Jim Lonborg of the Boston Red Sox who was injured in a skiing accident. The ruling said that any player injured in a non-baseball accident would not be paid for the time he missed during the season. It gave Fergie and other ballplayers pause for thought when indulging in other sports.

As the '68 season went on, Fergie's pitching continued to improve. In spite of a slow start, he ended the season with 20 wins, and the Cubs finished in third place. Everyone felt sure that the team would be a pennant contender next year. The season was one of "firsts" for Fergie. He was the first Chicago pitcher in 21 years to win 20 games in one season. He was also the first Canadian to achieve this since Russell Ford won 21 games in 1914 while playing for Buffalo in the Federal League.

Frank Lane, scouting for the Orioles, wouldn't talk about making a trade for Fergie. Instead, he said "Trade hell. I'd just like to kidnap that guy."

At about this time, *Sporting News* reported that Atlanta Braves player Marty Martinez seemed to be making all his roommates sick. One developed tuberculosis, another broke a finger then got hit in the face with a pitch that fractured his cheekbone, then another developed a kidney stone. When the team went to Chicago to play the Cubs, manager Luman Harris suggested that Martinez should find out where Fergie lived and go to stay with him for a while!

When Fergie signed his 1969 contract, there was a raise in store for him. He signed for $50,000, $15,000 more than the previous year. Negotiations had been held up by a dispute between the Baseball Players' Association and the club owners, and the Cubs' spring training camp was ten days late getting started. Fergie was waiting in Chicago to find out what was happening. As soon as he got word of the signing, he made a quick trip home to visit his parents, then was off to Scottsdale, Arizona.

At this time, the American League made a few changes to the game. For one thing, the mound was shaved from 15 inches to 10 inches. Fergie didn't feel it made a big difference to the pitchers, although he did have to adjust his delivery. The change, he felt, was more likely to benefit hitters.

"You have to accentuate your breaking pitches more from a low mound," he said at the time. " You have to pull down harder to make the ball break. If you have a tendency to overemphasize your fast ball, you might land on your heel with your front foot instead of on your toes. That will bring your fast ball too high and those hitters are going to jump on that high pitch." He added that there's not much ground to land on in front of a low mound, especially when you're 6'5".

Also that season, the strike zone as made smaller. Fergie didn't feel it made any difference to his game, nor was he concerned that the new balls seemed be smaller, lighter and "livelier." At about the same time, artificial turf was being put into ball parks all across the continent. The Astro turf was making the ball bounce faster and higher. Fergie's opinion was that in future, pitchers would be losing games in different ways than in the past.

"The new balls they are using...are wound much tighter and they really go when they are hit. With the new balls and the way the Astro turf is, you can just about bounce the baseball like an India rubber ball on cement," he observed.

The Cubs made their best start in 34 seasons, with Fergie blanking the St. Louis Cardinals 1-0. It looked like the beginning of a great year. Fergie felt that Durocher had confidence in him, seldom coming out to the mound to talk to him.

"He'll talk to me in the dugout sometimes, but he knows what I can do, and he lets me do it," Fergie told a reporter.

On one occasion when Durocher did talk to Fergie, Fergie said "No". It was before a home game when the Cubs were scheduled to come up against the Cincinnati Reds. Fergie had pitched on Sunday, and he was feeling tired. When Durocher asked him to pitch on Tuesday, he said "Two days rest just isn't enough. Honest, I'm tired." He begged off the mound again on Wednesday, but made up for it all on Thursday by hurling a 3-1 win over Cincinnati. The win broke the Cubs' four-game losing streak. A crowd of 29,092 fans turned out to see the game, bringing season attendance at Wrigley Field to 1,502,222, the biggest attendance since 1929.

Unfortunately, things did not continue to go well for the Cubs. Little more than a week later, Durocher gave Fergie a tongue-lashing in a pre-game meeting, calling him a "quitter" because the Cubs lost 13-4 to the Pittsburgh Pirates. As usual, Fergie took the criticism calmly, merely saying to the press , "I'm not a quitter. I've never quit on the Cubs and I did not quit Saturday."

The team faltered badly, and did not win the National League Pennant they had hoped for. September 9th, 1969 was the day that has gone down in history as an omen of the Cubs' bad luck that year. During a game against the New York Mets, a black cat wandered onto the field, walked in a complete circle around Ron Santo who was up at bat, then went back to the dugout where he stopped and, it is said, hissed at Durocher. It may have had nothing to do with bad luck; it may have been simply the psychological affect on the team, who couldn't help but notice the black cat. Certainly Durocher, who was known to be superstitious, noticed that black cat. The Cubs not only lost the game, but Fergie lost his 13th game of the season. After that, the Mets were hot and the Cubs were not. The Cubs ended the season eight games behind the Mets.

In spite of hard times, Fergie won 21 games that season. Nevertheless, Fergie still says that the '69 Cubs were one of the best teams he ever played with.

Asked if he was disappointed that the Cubs didn't win, P.K. Wrigley said "Naturally I'm disappointed....By now I'm used to disappointments."

There were plenty of disappointments in 1969 for Fergie, too. In spite of two consecutive 20-win seasons, he wasn't chosen for the National League All-Star team. Everyone thought he would be the pitcher, but team manager Red Schoendienst selected Ernie Banks for the spot instead. Even though he later said that Jenkins was his first choice, he had selected Banks at the suggestion of National League president Warren Giles. Fergie was a little surprised at being left out, and both fans and sportswriters expressed shock. As usual, though, Jenkins managed to accept the decision without any outward display of emotion.

Instead of brooding over his disappointment, Fergie went home to Chatham during the three-day All-Star break. While there, he found time to umpire first base in a Bantam League baseball game at Stirling Park near his parents' home.

Fans blamed Durocher for the Cubs' decline, at one game chanting "Good-bye, Leo, we hate to see you go!" In the end,

Durocher blamed himself, for he realized that he'd put too much pressure on his players, forced tired or injured players to get out there and play until they dropped. He realized too late that yelling and swearing did not get positive results with the team.

Still, Leo didn't change his tactics completely. He reached the point where he did not listen to either the players or his coaches. Sometimes he did not even post the lineup for the game until ten minutes before the game. Players couldn't prepare themselves in time to go onto the field and play effectively. Early in the 1970 season, the Cubs lost 12 consecutive games. It was embarassing. The Cubs had not made such a poor showing since 1944 when the club had dropped 13 games in a row. It was Ferguson Jenkins who pulled them out of the slump, beating the St. Louis Cardinals 5-0 at Busch Memorial Stadium. Fergie struck out 11 Cardinals, allowed only four hits, and walked just one man during this crucial game.

By the time that season ended, Fergie had passed the magic "20" mark, having won 20 games for the Cubs for the fourth year in a row. The achievement was all the more remarkable because it came just at a time of sorrow in Fergie's life. His mother, his guiding star, died of stomach cancer on September 15th, 1970, the same week of his 20th win of the season.

In 1971, Ron Santo got the idea that the Cubs should form a basketball team to keep in shape during the winter. Durocher didn't like the idea. He was always afraid that someone would get hurt and be unable to play when the baseball season opened. Eventually, though, he gave in to pressure, and even attended some of the teams' games. Still, the Cubs felt he was abandoning them, because he always walked out when the Cubs were not winning.

At the beginning of the 1971 season, everyone seemed to be dissatisfied with Leo. "Leo Must Go" buttons began to appear on lapels at the ballpark, and a Chicago newspaper ran a poll to see if readers thought he should stay on. Fans apparently voted in his favour, and even P. K. Wrigley announced that Leo would remain as manager of the Cubs.

After a clubhouse dustup with Ron Santo, Durocher stamped out of the locker room and up the stairs to telephone Wrigley and tell him he was quitting. Meanwhile, the players and management quickly agreed that it couldn't be allowed to happen. It didn't, but the rest of the season was a scaled down version of the Cold War.

Fergie plays basketball with the Cubs' off-season team

This was not a stellar period in Fergie's career. Among other things, he was the only pitcher in the big leagues to surrender home runs to all three of the Alou brothers. The occasions were in July, 1967 when Jesus Alou hit a homerun for the Giants, followed by Felipe's homer for the Braves in April, 1968, and Matty's for the Cardinals in September, 1971.

In May of 1971, Fergie almost lost his cool when umpire Dave Davidson called a balk on him. A balk is an incomplete or misleading motion on the part of the pitcher with one or more runners on base. Fergie said he was just leaning forward to get a better look at the catcher's sign to him when both the third base coach and the third base umpire called "balk".

"I've been in the National League five years and have been doing the same thing right along," Fergie fumed, "and now it's a balk."

Still on the whole, Fergie was satisfied with the way things were going. In fact, it was during this season that he pitched his 100th career win, when the Cubs trounced the Atlanta Braves 11-0. Always one to give credit where it was due, Fergie said of Randy Hundley "Having Hundley catch for you was like sitting down to a steak dinner with a steak knife. Without Hundley, all you had was a fork."

On another occasion, Fergie displayed his use of picturesque language in explaining why he didn't do better in an All-Star game.

"This is a hitter's park," he said, "but some of those home runs tonight would have been out of Yellowstone Park."

The 1971 season was also another 20-win year. *Globe and Mail* sportswriter Gord Walker noted that this was the earliest that Fergie had achieved the 20 mark. In 1967, the important date was September 29th; in 1968 it moved up a day to September 28th; in 1969 and 1970, it was September 17th and September 18th. In 1971, it jumped to August 20th.

To Fergie, the 20-win seasons were important personal landmarks, but not as important as the ultimate goal for the whole team, the pennant.

The 1972 season was no better for the Cubs. It was not bad for Fergie, though. The Cubs gave him a two-year contract for a total of $250,000. During the season, the National Film Board of Canada began shooting a film for Canadian audiences. The script dealt with Jenkins' career as an example of how a Canadian athlete could succeed in an American sport. The crew would turn up at various times in different cities where the team was playing. Several players were asked to participate by giving interviews, and all did so gladly - except Durocher. He seemed to resent the crew's intrusion into the team's regular schedule. It was said later that he asked for a large fee to be interviewed, and declined to appear when told that the budget didn't allow for such payments.

Fergie was at home in Chatham when he learned that Durocher had stepped down as the Cubs' manager. Although early reports said that P.K. Wrigley had fired him, the truth was that Leo had finally realized that the team would perform better under another manager. He had simply tried to get too much out of his players, and it backfired. He had resigned. He was too proud to wait until he was fired. No matter what the team or management thought of Durocher, the fact remains that he was wise enough to recognize Fergie Jenkins' potential, and give him the opportunity to go out onto the diamond and prove it.

When Carroll Walter 'Whitey' Lockman took over as the new manager, things began to go well for the club which won five of its first seven games. Lockman had a reputation as a "nice guy", but everyone knew he was a strong, dedicated person. Even so, the Cubs were known as a bunch of individualists who had difficulty working together as a team. Many team watchers wondered if he could pull the players together and make the team a force to be reckoned with. The press hinted that the team's better performance was due to Durocher's departure. For Fergie, the rest of the season was not stellar. He still managed to achieve another twenty wins by the end of the season, even though play got under way late due to a players' strike.

"Never in my wildest dreams did I think, six years ago, that I could win twenty games six years in a row," said Fergie at the time. The 1973 season started out as a good one for the Cubs. By the end of June, the club was 6½ games ahead. It looked as though the Cubs might make it all the way to the pennant. In spite of a sore knee, Fergie was pitching well.

Then everything went sour again. Team morale was at an all-time low. Fergie was disappointed with his own performance. At one point, he resorted to throwing bats around in the dugout in a rare display of anger at himself. Usually self-controlled whatever the circumstances, Fergie was obviously very frustrated. By the end of the season, Fergie had only 14 wins to his credit, along with 16 losses. There were rumours that he was "over the hill."

During this period, Fergie was suffering from tendonitis in his shoulder, the result of pitching so many innings for seven straight years. He tried cortisone shots to relieve the problem, but they didn't help much. He tried various exercise programs which helped but didn't completely cure the problem either. He knew

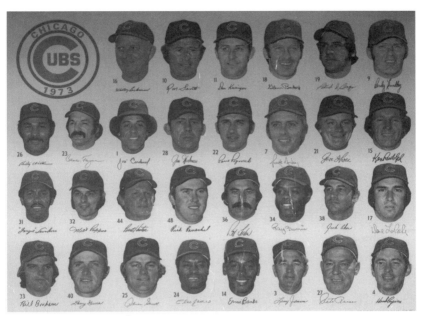

The 1973 Chicago Cubs

his performance was at a low ebb, and he badly wanted to improve it. He watched hours of films of himself pitching, trying to find the flaws so that he could correct them. He even changed his delivery, but that didn't help, either.

This was a difficult time for Fergie. After so much success, everything seemed to be going wrong. The fans booed him, and some even called him a bum and a quitter. It distressed him that his wife and two little girls often heard this. He stopped taking them to games. There was even a death threat in a letter sent to his home. Everything seemed to be falling apart. The Cubs management thought it might help if he were to see a psychiatrist at the University of Illinois. He did, in fact, find help in resolving his problems through talking about his mother's death, and other personal matters that had built up feelings of anger and guilt over the years.

At one point, the psychiatrist asked him if he had guns in his home. He said that he did. The doctor suggested that he lock them up. Fergie didn't think he was a danger to himself or anyone else, but he took the advice and locked up the guns. Still, his performance on the field did not improve much. Fergie, who was used to pitching every four days, found himself pitching only when manager Whitey Lockman told him to. This was often only every eight days. Fergie knew that to keep his skills honed, he needed to pitch more often than that.

Fergie had learned that fame and success can never be taken for granted. He felt that he was at rock bottom, bitter and lacking the self confidence that he had always had. Disheartened by his poor pitching average, he asked to be traded. The Cubs, it seems, had already come to the same conclusion. P.K. Wrigley had several highly paid players on his roster, and he couldn't afford to keep them when they weren't able to produce a pennant. Fergie at $125,000 a year was in that category.

At the time, Fergie commented that "If there'd been a team in Outer Mongolia, the Cubs would have sent me there." As far as the Cubs were concerned, Fergie was finished.

After lengthy negotiations, he was traded to the Texas Rangers in the American League in 1974.

12. A Change of Scene

Although Fergie was satisfied with the trade, both fans and the press were puzzled. The Rangers were expected to finish at the bottom of their division, and they had traded the hot young star, Bill Madlock for 30-year-old Fergie. It seemed like a mistake on the Rangers' part.

Writing in his book *The Wrong Stuff*, pitcher Bill Lee wrote, tongue in cheek, that "Fergie was traded to Texas for a couple of used baseballs and an autographed picture of Roy Rogers and Dale Evans." That was not true, of course, but the suggestion was pretty humiliating.

As far as Jenkins was concerned, the move was a challenge. The Cubs had said he was all washed up in the big leagues. He was getting "old". He had a bad back and a bad arm. The Cubs may have thought they were putting him out to pasture.

People like Fergie, however, are motivated by adversity. The change of scene to Arlington, Texas made him feel rejuvenated. He set out to prove that none of the negatives things said about him were true.

For one thing, during the off-season, he went home to Chatham. His aim was to relax and take a good look at himself. He spent a lot of time talking to Kathy and to his father. At last he felt able to pour out to them all the things that had been bothering him over the last few years. Putting those issues into words also brought them into focus for him, and he was able to deal with them. By the time he began playing for the Rangers, the worst of it was behind him.

As it turned out, it was not a bad deal for the Rangers after all. In fact, it seemed to be a replay of Fergie's trade from the Phillies to the Cubs: the appearance at first of a bad deal for the new club, followed by a sense of regret by the old one. At the beginning of the season, the Texas team was expected to finish at the bottom of its league. Under the circumstances, some fans and sportswriters were surprised at first that the team had given up Bill Madlock for the aging Fergie. However, Fergie started out pitching beautifully,

On the mound, Fergie confers with manager Billy Martin of the Texas Rangers

Fergie in action with the Rangers, with Pat Kelly up to bat

It's crowded in the dugout - Fergie has to lean on Billy Martin's shoulder to chat

and the Texas fans loved him.

Reggie Jackson of the Oakland A's was impressed with Fergie's performance. He was quoted as saying, "The guy that got rid of him in Chicago ought to be fired."

In April and May of that year, he pitched six wins, one loss, and struck out seven batters. In his second and third games, he enjoyed scores of 10-2. He told reporters "I didn't know what to do with that many runs. That was about eight games worth when I was with the Cubs."

That wasn't just a "sour grapes" reaction on Fergie's part. He had worked hard for the Cubs, and often didn't get the runs he deserved to back him up. One game in Atlanta during the 1968 season, he had pitched ten scoreless innings, until he finally felt his shoulder tiring, and had to tell Leo Durocher that he'd had enough. The Cubs lost 1-0 in the 11th inning. Two days later, he went ten innings again. When he left the field, the score was 3-3. Again, the Cubs lost in the 11th inning. By the end of that week, Fergie was exhausted, and had no wins to show for it.

In spite of a mid-season slump in his first season with the Rangers, he finished the season with 25 wins and only 12 losses. It was his seventh 20-win season in eight years, and during a game with the Cleveland Indians he chalked up his 2000th strikeout. The Rangers finished second to the world champion Oakland Athletics. Not only that, but attendance was at an all-time high. Many observers thought that Fergie was a candidate to win the Cy Young Award for the American League, but it went to Catfish Hunter of Oakland instead.

In 1974, still playing with the Rangers, Ferguson Jenkins was voted the American League's Comeback Player of the Year.

With typical humility, Fergie placed credit for his astonishing comeback in two places. First of all, he rediscovered his faith in God. It was something that had been with him all his life, but in the years since his mother's death, he had allowed it to become eclipsed by so many negative forces around him. He talked it out with Kathy, and decided to get back to going to church and to become more involved with the Fellowship of Christian Athletes. The other source of his renewed inspiration came from Ranger manager Billy Martin who recognized the difficult time Fergie was having and gave him back confidence in himself and his performance as a pitcher. It certainly worked. At the end of the season, his lawyer negotiated a new contract for him. It was for one year only, but it brought him a raise to $175,000

It was during this period, when living in Texas, that Fergie adopted the cowboy hat as his trade mark headwear. When he moved to the ranch in Oklahoma, it continued to be practical. At public appearances, Fergie can quickly be identified, both by his height and by his hat which is nearly always on his head or somewhere nearby. When sitting down, he places it on the floor, brim-side up. "You're supposed to do that," he explains to anyone who tries to turn it over.

Among top ballplayers, Fergie was one of those known to media people as a "go-to guy". He could be relied on to talk to them and tell it to them straight. On one occasion, the Texas Rangers were annoyed at the media for some reason, and no one on the team would speak to the press. Mike Bennett, sports director for the *Chatham Daily News* recalls that Fergie and Al Oliver rose above the situation, went up to the press box and smoothed over the situation.

The Buffalo Head Gang

13. The Buffalo Head Gang

The Rangers traded Fergie Jenkins to the Boston Red Sox in 1976. That was the only year in which he spent time on the DL - Disabled List. Players dislike being on the DL, and Jenkins was no exception. He wasn't used to being laid up with injuries. Idleness was an annoying inconvenience.

"I never iced my arm," he said at the time, "and I think I had one cortisone shot in my life." In 1976, the injury was an Achilles tendon tear in the right heel. It was very painful, and it meant that he had to spend six months in rehab before being able to get back into the game. Never one to enjoy inactivity, Fergie resented being unable to play, and was eager to get back into the game.

During the period in Boston, he was identified with a group of rebels within the team, a group of "bad guys" known as the Buffalo Heads. The Buffalo Head Gang was a group of five including Fergie, Bill "Space Man" Lee, Bernie Carbo, Rick Wise and Jim Willoughby - four pitchers and an infielder. Their lockers were together at the back of the change room. They seemed to have a lot in common, and they became close friends, frequently socializing after practice or a game. One of the things they had in common was a dislike of coach Don Zimmer. He did not seem to like them, either.

"You have to understand," Bill Lee says, "That the reason for the existence of the Buffalo Heads is that we were being mistreated." Asked in what way were they mistreated, he explains "We were misunderstood. We were a group of pitchers being managed by little middle infielders who know only one thing about pitching, and that is that it is hard to hit."

At that time, groups of sightseers were sometimes taken on tours of the locker room. Fergie had *Playboy* centrefolds in his locker, and on one occasion he came into the locker room to find towels hung over the locker to screen the centrefolds from the eyes of a tour group which had come through. Fergie protested this. He felt that his locker was his personal space, and it was no one's business what pictures were in it. Fergie exchanged words with

Don Zimmer over the incident. Zimmer, sometimes referred to as 'Popeye" because of his strength, was not always a favourite with the players.

A couple of weeks later, the *Boston Globe* ran an article about Zimmer, and published an accompanying cartoon of him with a huge head, and stick body, arms and legs. Everyone got a great kick out of it, except Zimmer. Fergie cut out the picture and pinned it up in his locker with the words Buffalo Head printed across the bottom. When asked why Buffalo Head, he gave his teammates a cock-and-bull story, saying that the picture reminded him of the buffalo that the Indians used to drive over the Niagara Escarpment. Bill Lee who refers to himself as the patron saint or philosopher king of

Fergie walking on the beach with his two-year-old daughter Kelly.

the Buffalo Heads, recalls that Fergie commented that the buffalo was the dumbest animal on earth. The description seemed to fit. Lee says that as a result of Fergie's story about the buffalo being driven over the cliff, he travelled all the way to Head- Smashed-In Buffalo Jump, about 10 miles northwest of Fort McLeod in Alberta to see the real thing for himself. Incidentally, Native Canadians did drive buffalo herds over cliffs as a convenient method of hunting. However, it never happened at the Niagara Escarpment; the buffalo didn't roam there. Fergie's comment was just an Adelaide Street Gang type of joke.

At the time, the Boston team was a good solid contending team. It was about time, for the Red Sox were in a long dry spell that some said was the result of "the curse". The Boston team won the first World Series held in 1903, and during the next 15 years they won again four more times. Then in 1919, the owner, Harry Frazee traded Babe Ruth to the Yankees for $100,000 and a $300,000 mortgage on Fenway Park to fund his other passion, Broadway musicals. Ruth had hit a phenomenal 29 homeruns during the 1919 season, but there was contention over his salary. After he was traded, Ruth went on to a stellar career in baseball, while the Boston team had never been a contender for the World Series. Now things were looking up.

The Buffalo Heads had all come from different clubs, but they were working together well for the Red Sox. Then, one at a time, they fell out of favour with Zimmer. Fergie was told that he

Fergie and the Texas Rangers meet the New York Yankees in Yankee Stadium

couldn't beat any team. He, Bill Lee and Rich Wise were all relegated to the bullpen; Bernie Carbo, the best outfielder on the team, wasn't allowed on the field. Jim Willoughby who was leading the team in ERA wasn't allowed to pitch. At the end of the season, the Red Sox were beaten out of the championships by the Yankees.

"It was really too bad," Fergie says. "When we were on the road, we went to the racetrack and out to eat with Don, and we had great times. But when you put on that uniform, it was different. I think he really didn't think pitchers were as important as hitters."

The Buffalo Heads were definitely an unusual group. As each one was traded away from Boston, remaining members of the group surreptitiously crept into Zimmer's office and put a lighted candle on the desk "in memory of the dear departed souls".

Bill Lee and Fergie hold an autographed sketch of the Buffalo Head Gang as they appeared in 1976, and as they looked 20 years later.

"I really enjoyed pitching at Fenway Park," Fergie recalls. "I was used to pitching at Wrigley Field which is also small." Fenway is a popular ballpark with both fans and players. It has a homey, intimate atmosphere that everyone loves. This is partly due to the fact that it was built to fit into a neighbourhood that had streets that met on odd angles rather than at right angles. The park's name, Fenway, is a tribute to the fact that it was built on a marshy part of Boston known as The Fens.

The park's past is loaded with history, too. On opening day, 1912, the first pitch was thrown out by John F. Kennedy's grandfather, John Fitzgerald who was mayor of Boston. This was the first time that the national anthem had been played at the beginning of a game, and it was the start of a tradition.

The 1980-81 seasons were plagued by strikes. Fergie Jenkins and other Boston players were involved. Players were asking for a raise in pay. The club owners were crying poor, saying that they couldn't afford to pay more, and that permitting players to become free agents was ruining baseball. They made it sound as though the players were a very greedy bunch indeed. The players, on the other hand, felt that the owners were making plenty of money and were being unfair in their refusal to pay more. The 1981 season was cut short by the strike, and Fergie only managed five wins that year.

According to law, the clubs didn't have to open their books; they were private corporations. So when the players asked for more money, and the dispute went to arbitration, the independent arbitrators almost always took the players' part. They assumed that the owners really did have the money. So salaries escalated. To quote one former player, "An owner is a guy who has a gun with lots of bullets, and he's always shooting himself in the foot." Perhaps if the owners had willingly opened their books, arbitrators could have seen where they really stood, and many of the difficulties could have been prevented. Also, the escalation of players' salaries to today's huge levels might never have got started.

While never one to look for trouble, Ferguson Jenkins supported the strike. "We would be lost without the Association

[Major League Ball Players Association]," he said. "We're like a bunch of floundering idiots without it." Fergie had nothing to gain from the strike. He was getting close to retirement, and would never make the huge salaries that younger players were destined to receive. As always, he was in favour of fairness.

During the down time of the 1981 strike, *Inside Sports* magazine did a study of pitchers, based on their ratio of strikes-outs to walks. Fergie led the pack, with such big names as Christy Mathewson, Sandy Koufax and Dizzy Dean trailing far behind.

During the strike, Fergie kept in shape by working out regularly. He knew by now that it would be a mistake to slack off even for a short time.

In 1982, Fergie was traded back to the Chicago Cubs where he redeemed himself by making a good showing. By the end of that season, he had 278 pitching wins to his credit. The following year, he was quoted in the *Wall Street Journal* as saying. "My arm never felt better, so that's no problem. When I have my Cubs uniform on, it thinks its twenty-five."

In spite of feeling that he was in good shape, things didn't always go well. After giving up six runs in a single inning in one game, he was quoted in *The Sporting News* as saying "I thought I was throwing OK. So did the hitters, I guess."

By the time Fergie turned 40 in 1983, he was thinking of retiring. His friend and mentor, Gene Dziadura, thought he had one or two more good seasons left in him, but in spite of Gene's encouragement, Fergie decided to retire.

"My kids were growing up," he says, "and it seemed like a good time to come home to Chatham." The Cubs were thinking "young", and when Fergie went to spring training, he was the oldest pitcher there. He knew that if he stayed on, he would be traded. Although prestigous names like the Dodgers and the Yankees were mentioned, his loyalty remained with the Cubs. He just didn't want to be uprooted again.

Fergie Jenkins retired as club leader in strikeouts with 274 in one season, and a total of 2,036 throughout his career with the Cubs. He was only the fourth pitcher in history to win more than

100 games in both leagues. The first three to earn this distinction were Cy Young, Jim Bunning and Gaylord Perry. Only two more have been added to this exceptional list since. They were Nolan Ryan and Dennis Martinez.

Jenkins is the only pitcher in history to record more than 3,000 strikeouts - 3,192, to be exact - while at the same time giving up less than 1,000 walks - only 997. He defeated 24 different teams at least six times each! He beat the Phillies 26 times, and the Cardinals 19 times. Nothing is ever perfect, of course. Pittsburgh defeated Jenkins 23 times, and although he pitched against the Cubs and the Rangers during his career, he never succeeded in winning against these teams. Three times he was runner-up in Pitching's Triple Crown Contenders points in the National League.

It was an illustrious 21-year career, one he could be proud of. Wrigley Field, Fergie's home park while he was with the Cubs, is a batter's dream, a pitcher's nightmare. Known as one of the most beautiful ball parks on the continent, it is a small field compared to some others, seating only about 39,000 fans. Batters find it easy to hit the ball right out of the park, especially when the wind is blowing out of the park. Also, behind the pitcher is a brick wall covered with ivy, planted back in 1937 by Bill Veech during a renovation of the park. The white ball stands out against the background so that the batter can easily see it. Only when the wind is blowing into the park does the field favour pitchers. One of the reasons for Jenkins' success in Wrigley Field, was his tremendous control. Whether he was throwing a slider, a change-up, a curveball or a fastball, he could always put the ball across the outside corner of the plate.

Fans love Wrigley Field; it epitomizes baseball and America itself.

The history of the park goes back to 1914 when it was created for Charlie Weeghman's Federal League team. It was originally called North Side Ball Park, but the name was soon changed to Weeghman Park, then to Whales Park after the Federal League team. In 1916, Weegham and his associates purchased the Cubs, and the name was changed once again to Cubs Park. In 1918, Weegham sold the controlling interest in the Cubs to William Wrigley Jr. It wasn't until 1926 that the park became known as Wrigley Field.

After every game, even those who didn't attend immediately know how it turned out. A white flag with a "W" flies aloft on the field after every win; a blue flag with an "L" tells of a loss.

14. The Cy Young Award

Every young baseball player dreams of reaching the Big Leagues. After that, if he's a pitcher, his next dream is to win the Cy Young Award. Who was Cy Young? Why is this honour so coveted by the baseball elite?

Denton True Young became one of the early heroes of baseball. He was born near Gilmore, Ohio in 1867. He quit school after Sixth Grade and worked on the family farm. Far from stagnating in these surroundings, he found a passionate love - baseball. On local teams, his fastball quickly earned him the nickname Cy, short for Cyclone. The Cleveland Spiders of the National League picked up his contract for $300.

These were the days when he was pitching against legends like Amos Rusie, Bill Hutchinson and Kid Nicholas. He did it so well that the team - and its opponents - were impressed. So were the fans.

Young's early days on the diamond were in a different baseball era. Until 1896, Young never used a glove. Nor, for many years, would he play on a Sunday. Pitchers threw the ball underhand, yet Young's pitching could provide an exciting challenge for the hitter. By 1896, Young was known as the premier pitcher in baseball. He began to change his thinking, by this time using a glove and agreeing to participate in Sunday games. More than once, he served as umpire when the need arose.

Young moved up through the leagues, to the St. Louis Perfectos and the Boston Red Sox. The first World's Series was held in 1903, with Boston pitted against the Pittsburgh Pirates, and Young hurling from the mound. It was a victory for Boston.

Cy Young became the grand old man of baseball, continuing to pitch in the National league until 1912 when his arm finally gave out. He was the first pitcher to win 500 games, and by the time he retired, he had a total of 511 wins. He was one of the early inductees into the Cooperstown Baseball Hall of Fame, being elected in 1937 with 153 votes out of the 201 ballots cast. He was among the first celebrities to donate memorabilia to the Hall. He

The late Jim Enwright of the Chicago Daily News presents the Cy Young Award to Fergie at the start of the 1972 season at Wrigley Field.

died in 1955, aged 89.

An award for the best pitcher in the major leagues was the idea of Commissioner Ford Frick. The award was to be named in honour of Cy Young, and the winner was to be chosen by a panel from the Baseball Writers' Association of America. The first award was presented in 1956 to Don Newcombe of the Brooklyn Dodgers. Frick was adamant that only one winner should be chosen from the National and American Leagues. However, when Frick retired in 1966, the rules were changed. From then on, the best pitcher in each league was honoured each year.

Like other pitchers, Ferguson Jenkins was eager to join the list of all-time pitching greats. His first full season as a regular pitcher was 1967, the first time he won 20 games in a single season. In that year, he got one vote for the Cy Young award; Mike McCormick got 18 of the 20 remaining votes. Apparently, one judge had noticed that Jenkins' pitching was responsible for the Cubs' move up from the bottom of the league to third place.

Fergie was disappointed that he didn't get more votes, but that was mitigated by the fact that he was chosen one of the three Outstanding Young Men of Ontario by the Ontario Jaycees. He was the first black person to be selected for the award.

The following year, Fergie won 20 games again, but Bob Gibson got the coveted Cy Young Award that year. In 1969, Jenkins once again had a 20-win season, but in spite of that, he got no votes. In 1970, he placed third in the voting, with 16 points compared to winner Gibson's 118.

At last it was Ferguson Jenkins' turn to win for the National League in 1971. After five consecutive twenty-win seasons, he knew he deserved it. He was delighted to learn that he had won the prestigious award, but at the same time, he was surprised as well. "I knew I had a pretty good year," he said. "but quite a few other pitchers in the league had a good year, too."

He knew he had earned this recognition, but he also gave credit for his success to the Cubs' former pitching coach Joe Becker. While Gene Dziadura had laid the groundwork with Fergie's pitching mechanics, Becker had helped him refine it.

"I wish he was back," Fergie was quoted as saying. "He said if I worked hard, I'd get a lot of benefit. He took my windup away and gave me a shorter windup. And if he shouted at you, you knew you were doing wrong. If he smiled, you knew you were going great." Fergie gave Becker credit for telling him to get out there and pitch every fourth day, to throw hard, throw strikes and to concentrate all the time. If he followed that advice, Becker said, Fergie would make a million dollars in baseball.

Becker had a lot of confidence in Fergie's ability. He could see a few things that needed to be fixed, but he knew that they would be easy to remedy. For example, he quickly saw that Fergie was tipping his pitches by dangling his right arm by his right knee when he was taking the sign. The batter could see how he was holding the ball, and knew which pitch to expect.

Becker told a *Toronto Star* reporter in detail about Fergie's pitch, saying that "he wasn't driving in with his left shoulder. He had to get that left shoulder pointed right at the batter, and drive it at him when he threw. Otherwise, he's throwing with his arm, not his body. Also, he was coming around open-armed a lot, swinging out when he should be swinging in...I just got him shoving off on that back foot. Then he gets the support of his hips, the left shoulder digs in, and now he's a pitcher."

Fergie took every one of these suggestions to heart. Now, he

Fergie with all six balls and gloves from his 20-game consecutive winning seasons.

seemed to be on the way to that million dollars.

Of 24 sportswriters polled in 12 National League cities in 1971, 17 gave Jenkins their first-place vote. Tom Seaver of the New York Mets got six votes, and Al Downing of the Los Angeles Dodgers got the other. Fergie also received three second place votes and three third place votes. Of the 24 ballots cast, he was mentioned on all but one, and he won an amazing 97 points in the scoring. The point system gave five points for each first place vote, three for a second, and one for a third. It was a landslide vote of confidence from the Baseball Writers' Association of America.

Ferguson Jenkins became the first Canadian and the first Chicago Cub to win the coveted Cy Young Award.

A little of the pleasure was rubbed off when Tom Seaver, who had won the award in 1969, showed obvious disappointment. It wasn't only the fact that he lost that upset Seaver, but the fact that he lost by so much when he had just completed a good season. He trailed Jenkins with only 61 points in the Cy Young voting.

The coveted trophy was presented first at a big banquet in New York City. Then, for the benefit of fans, it was presented again at Wrigley Field before the All-Star game in Chicago.

Jenkins deserved the award, though. For the fifth year in a row, he had won 20 games. No pitcher had done that since Warren Spahn's winning record with the Milwaukee Braves between 1956 and 1960. In 1971, Fergie had led the National League in wins and complete games.

During that season, he pitched 305 innings, yielded just 37 walks, and accumulated 263 strikeouts. He was the Cubs' all-time leader in strikeouts with a total of 1,466. It didn't hurt, either, that he was a good hitter for a pitcher, hitting .245 with 24 runs batted in and six home runs during the season.

It was the first time a Chicago Cub had won the Cy Young Award, and it gave Fergie some leverage in asking for a raise. There were reports in the press that he was asking for $150,000 a year or even $200,000, but Fergie laughed off those reports. He left the bargaining to his lawyers. While the money was important in the sense that it brought recognition, he wasn't interested in a lavish lifestyle. His family, his farm and his dogs were of more importance. In the end, he settled for $90,000. More was in store, however. For the 1972 and 1973 seasons, he signed a contract for $125,000 a year. The Chicago Cubs had never before had a player so highly paid, and few pitchers had ever reached that level.

In spite of this, Fergie didn't get the publicity he deserved. Even the *Chicago Defender*, Chicago's leading black newspaper, didn't give him much coverage, except on one occasion to observe that "the only time anyone notices Ferguson Jenkins is when something goes wrong." Nor did advertisers rush to invite him to endorse their products. Many sports celebrities make considerable extra income from endorsements, but this opportunity never came Fergie's way.

As for the Cy Young Award itself, the trophy is a beautiful piece of artwork. Unfortunately, it is not to be found in Jenkins' trophy cases at the ranch, although he does have a replica. Some years ago, the owner of a New York City restaurant asked if he could borrow the trophy to display with other sports memorabilia in his establishment. Fergie was naturally flattered by the request, and trustingly handed over the trophy. Some time later, he returned to the restaurant, thinking it was time to reclaim his prized possession. To his horror, the restaurant had changed hands. The décor had changed, and the new owner knew nothing about items that were in the premises before he took over. Fergie set about trying to trace the previous owner. It was a paper chase, with Fergie never seeming to be able to catch up with the man. He eventually learned that the restaurant owner had sold the trophy to a collector.

Finally, Jenkins heard that the Cy Young trophy was in the hands of actor Charlie Sheen. He asked a mutual acquaintance to approach Sheen and ask if he could have the trophy back. Reportedly, Sheen's reply was "Sure, but it will cost him."

Fergie just can't accept the idea of paying to get his own trophy back, especially when it was taken from him and sold without his permission in the first place. To add insult to injury, his wife learned through an internet website that Fergie was rumoured to have sold the trophy for $25,000!

"It's priceless to me," he said. "There's no way I'd sell it for that kind of money, or for any other amount either."

Once again, in 1974, Jenkins was a contender for the Cy Young Award in the American League. In spite of a great season - he won four 1-0 games - he was beaten out in the voting by Jim 'Catfish' Hunter. He was just two points behind. Gaylord Perry was the only pitcher to win the Cy Young Award in both leagues, and it would have been a feather in Fergie's cap to have matched the honour. If he was disappointed, however, he didn't show it in public. Instead, in speaking to the press, he pointed out that Hunter was playing for a first place club, and had a lot going for him. The response was typical of Fergie. He is matter-of-fact in his assessment of situations, and rarely speaks ill of anyone. That accounts for his continuing popularity with fans and players alike.

Even before the Cy Young Award, Fergie had had a satisfying relationship with the Baseball Writers Association of America. In 1967, he was invited to the annual Diamond Dinner (a $15 dollar a plate affair) hosted by the BBWAA's Chicago Chapter to receive a trophy as one of the Chicago Players of the Year. The other one was Joe Horlen of the Chicago White Sox. Canada's Centennial Year, 1967, was also a landmark year for Ferguson Jenkins.

Back in his days in Chicago, Fergie's popularity won him a spot on a local radio station. Six days a week, he got up in time to be at the studio at 7.55 a.m. for a five-minute commentary on baseball. A local school teacher who went to school with Fergie's mother is recorded as saying she liked to listen to him because "his English is so good."

Even before the Cy Young Award, Fergie's reputation as a pitcher earned him an opportunity to try his hand at writing. Both the *Windsor Star* and the *London Evening Free Press* published a weekly column entitled "Fergie Jenkins...on Baseball". Written in a casual style, the column gave tips for ballplayers and related interesting stories of Fergie's experiences.

In one column, Fergie wrote that he thought that baseball would be easier than high school. When he signed that first

Phillies contract, he thought he was through learning. He soon discovered how wrong he was! In spring training, several days were spent just learning the team signs which proved to be very complicated. Moves such as touching a face mask, wiping a hand on a pant leg, dropping a finger all give specific instructions and must be remembered.

Fergie also had another foray into the field of writing, preparing an instructional manual entitled *Inside Pitching*. The success of both these ventures proves that Ferguson Jenkins is a man of many talents and interests, as well as a good manager of the time at his disposal.

15. The Accolades Continue

Fergie's success on the mound was attributed to a "rubber arm". It just didn't seem to get sore, although by the end of the 1971 season, both the arm and it's owner were ready for a rest.

With the Cy Young Award and seven years in the National League under his belt, Fergie felt ready for a good many more years on the mound. That he was just hitting his stride was proved in February, 1972 when he was named Pitcher of the Year at the Sixth Annual Braves '400' Club Eddie Glennon Gameboree.

The same year, when the *Sporting News* polled National League players, Jenkins was chosen as pitcher for the All-Star team. He, along with third baseman Joe Torres who was selected as Player of the Year, were presented with engraved Bulova Accutron wristwatches.

On Monday, February 7th, 1972, the city of London, Ontario, rolled out the official red carpet for Ferguson Jenkins Day. The celebrations began with the presentation of a scroll by Mayor J. Fred Gosnell, and continued with the 25th Annual Sportsmen's Dinner. The latter event was held regularly to raise money for the London and District Crippled Children's Treatment Centre. As always, Fergie graciously participated in this gathering of Canadian and U.S. sports celebrities.

When the Chatham Kiwanis Club hosted a similar event at the Holiday Inn, municipal bigwigs turned out in force to show their support for their hometown hero. Members of Council, the water commission, the hydro commission and the administration staff of the city all joined Kiwanians for the occasion. Mayor Doug Allin, who had been one of Fergie's coaches during his early sandlot days in Chatham, gave the keynote speech.

In part, he said "In those days, he wasn't putting forth his all, and one hot day he was told to start running around the ballpark. We forgot about him, and about an hour later, he asked if he had run enough. That was his first lesson in obedience, a lesson he never forgot." While the exercise was good for Fergie, he didn't really need to learn obedience. It was something that he had been learning all his life from parents who had a lot of love, but high expectations for him, too.

Everyone in Chatham was proud of the city's hero, and eager to give him recognition. Branch 421 of the Canadian Legion made Fergie an honorary member, presenting him with a coveted Legion jacket.

Among his many honours seldom mentioned was that of being named a member of the prized Order of Canada. His appointment was announced on December 17th, 1979, and Fergie travelled to Rideau Hall in Ottawa to attend the investiture ceremony. The Order of Canada was instituted on July 1, 1967, the 100th anniversary of Confederation. The appointments are made by the governor-general, and are based on the recommendation of an advisory council which considers nominations submitted by members of the public.

Besides being a great honour for any Canadian - the award is made for "distinguished service in or to a particular locality, group or field activity" - the badge is a beautiful snowflake design. It is worn around the neck with a red and white ribbon, and a small replica can also be worn on street clothes. Jenkins is now entitled to use the letters CM after his name, although he never does.

Unlike many of the big names in sports, he has never been standoffish or unwilling to share his time for events of this nature. Whether the appearance was scheduled for a high profile city event or a small town gathering, he always agreed amiably when his schedule permitted.

Fergie has always been especially delighted to sign autographs for children. Even in the days when crowds of kids waited for him to come out of the Cubs' dressing room at Wrigley Field, he took time with them, even if it meant being late for something else. He's still the same in the year 2002.

At one time, it bothered Fergie that American sports writers knew so little about Canada. When Montreal got the National League franchise, one sportswriter said "I suppose you'll have a lot of Canadian fans on your side when the Cubs play Montreal. Guess that's not far from your home, eh?" He was surprised when

Fergie told him Montreal was a big city, 600 miles from his hometown. He pointed out that Montreal had (at that time) a larger population than such National League cities as Pittsburgh, Cincinnati and Atlanta. When he told teammates that Texas would fit into Ontario almost three times, they couldn't believe it. Most hadn't the faintest idea of the geography of southern Ontario, let alone Canada as a whole. Fergie threatened to send for maps and brochures to educate his teammates.

When it was suggested that Fergie might want to get traded to Montreal, Durocher nipped that idea in the bud. "He's one guy they don't get!" Leo said emphatically. *Macleans Magazine* did include Fergie in its list of possible Canadian players for the new team, although Montreal's general manager, Jim Fanning was reported as saying regretfully "I doubt it he'll be available."

When the newly rebuilt Montreal Forum opened in November, 1968, Ferguson Jenkins was one of the celebrities invited to the glittering, Hollywood-style event. The Forum was the home of the Montreal Canadiens, and as a lover of hockey, Fergie was happy to be there. When introduced with the other celebrities at centre ice, he got a huge ovation. After the ribbon-cutting ceremony featuring Quebec Premier Jean-Jacques Bertrand, Fergie and a crowd of 18,114 watched the Canadiens beat the Detroit Red Wings 2-1.

In 1974, there was talk of the World Baseball Association operating franchises in Toronto and Vancouver. Fergie's lawyers negotiated with WBA officials in Washington in the hopes that he might come home to play professional baseball in Canada. However, nothing ever came of it.

Another phase of Fergie's life that is seldom mentioned was his brief foray into the world of politics. During the height of his pitching career, when he was one of the most famous citizens of southwestern Ontario, he was persuaded to run for the Liberal Party in a provincial election. The party was looking for candidate to parachute into a Windsor riding where they had no one to run against the incumbent. They wanted someone who was recognizable and popular. It was flattering to be asked, and Fergie agreed to run. It was difficult to step into a community where he didn't know the issues, so in spite of his personal popularity, he didn't take the seat. However, Fergie has always been interested in community affairs and local politics. He has said that he would run for municipal office if the opportunity ever arose. He felt that he could do a lot for Chatham as its mayor. This is one dream that he has not achieved so far.

16. Harlem Globetrotters

Back in 1926, young Abe Saperstein organized and coached a basketball team which he called the Savoy Five. The team was sponsored by the Savoy Ballroom in Chicago, a favourite dance spot that the owners thought might be come even more attractive if it offered a basketball game as an added attraction. The team's career at the Savoy didn't last long, but Saperstein knew a good thing when he saw it. The following year, he reorganized his team and renamed it the Harlem Globetrotters. The players wore jerseys with the words "New York" on them, to give the impression that they were from the Big Apple. It wasn't until 46 years later that the team actually played a game in Harlem.

The Globetrotters made their official debut in Hinckley, Illinois on January 7th, 1927. A crowd of 300 turned out to see them. From then on, the team travelled in Saperstein's Ford Model T, bringing fun and excitement to audiences all across the continent. Their games were recognized by basketball fans and fun-lovers alike as exhibitions of outstanding skill. When the NBA finally decided to sign black players, the New York Knicks purchased Nathaniel "Sweetwater" Clifton's contract from the Globetrotters.

Abe Saperstein died in 1966 at age 63. However, the team was far from finished. It was purchased the following year by sportsmen Potter Palmer IV, John O'Neil and George Gilbert Jr. This happened to be the 40th anniversary for the team, and the occasion was celebrated by a game played where it all began - Hinckley, Illinois. At the same time, the new owners wanted to add something extra to the appearances. They came up with the idea of working celebrities from other sports into their games. Ferguson Jenkins Jr. was one of these.

In 1967, the team was scheduled to tour Canada. George Gillett, the general manager for the Globetrotters, delegated Canadian Wendell Smith of the *Chicago Sun-Times* to approach Fergie with a proposal. Jenkins jumped at the chance. Of course he had to try out for the team, but he held his own. With the blessing of John Holland of the Chicago Cubs, he signed on the dotted line. The agreement was that he would appear in a skit in each game, and play three or four minutes with the team. Fergie would gladly have played longer in each game, but Cubs wanted

Fergie balances a baseball on a basketball during a 1967 promotion for the Globetrotters. With Globetrotters general manager George Gillette, on left, and Hallie Bryant, on right.

to be sure that he didn't sustain an injury that would prevent him playing in the spring.

So during the 1967 off-season, Jenkins was hired to go on ahead of the team, doing radio, television and newspaper interviews, and posing for photos in a Globetrotter uniform as advance publicity for the appearances. He joined the club in Vancouver and travelled eastwards with them. Originally scheduled to play seven games with the team, he ended up playing eleven, seven of them in Canada. Fergie had turned out to be a real crowd attraction, especially at Globetrotter games in the Chicago area where he was already popular. On the tour across Canada, the

Fergie with Harlem Globetrotter founder Abe Saperstein

team stopped at London, Kitchener, Toronto, Kingston, Montreal, Sherbrooke, with one game in Buffalo.

Fergie was billed as an added attraction - "The pitcher who gives up a home run - every night."

During the games, Fergie would sit on the bench until sometime in the third quarter when Meadowlark Lemon would yell "Hey, we have a famous Chicago pitcher in the crowd! Let's play a ballgame." They would "coax" Fergie out onto the floor where he would wind up and roll the ball to Meadowlark. That would be Strike One. Then he'd throw the ball and hit Meadowlark. The umpire would yell "Strike Two". Next Fergie would throw the ball to Lemon who would hit it into the stands for a home run. Sometimes Showboat Hall would take over the skit instead of Lemon, but the crowds always loved it. After all, it was a pitcher's nightmare to give up a homerun in every game. On other occasions, the team devised other skits such as Around The World or Out-of-Bounds. The crowds loved it.

Somewhere along the line, it was discovered that Fergie was a pretty good basketball player. After all, it had been one of his first loves in sports. In a game in Montreal, before a crowd of 12,000 fans, he scored ten points for the Globetrotters.

The following season, the celebrity attraction was featured again, and Fergie played in 85 games. The tour this time took the team all across Canada and the United States, as well as to Hawaii.

Jenkins remembers that period fondly. This was a fairly profitable period for Jenkins. He got paid for doing the advance publicity for the team, and also for playing in the games. Besides, it was fun.

The Globetrotters travelled with the New York Generals, and the two teams played each other at appearances. Although the teams travelled on separate buses, there was a closeness between the two groups that created pleasant memories.

Fergie Jenkins was not the only baseball player to travel with the Harlem Globetrotters on similar terms. Others before him were Bob Gibson, Ernie Banks, Willie Mays and Frank Robinson. However, it's unlikely that anyone else enjoyed the tour more than Fergie did. After all, basketball was his "first choice" sport.

17. The National Baseball Hall of Fame

Inductees into the National Baseball Hall of Fame at Cooperstown, New York, are chosen by ten-year members of the Baseball Writers' Association of America. Each year, members of the BBWAA can vote for no more than ten players who become eligible five years after retirement; the players remain on the ballot for 15 years.

In 1989, his fifth year after retirement, and again in 1990, Ferguson Jenkins' name was on the ballot of players in the running for admission to the Baseball Hall of Fame. On both occasions, he came up short of votes. In 1989, he was fifth, with a 102-vote deficit; 333 votes were needed for a player to attain the 75% needed. The following year, he did better, with 296 votes, just 37 short of the number required for induction. It's true that in both 1989 and 1990, Fergie was up against some of baseball's mega-stars in the voting. Some of them had the advantage of having been on consistently winning teams, and of being more recognizable to the general public through endorsements and television commercials.

Fergie was disappointed. So were his fans back in southwestern Ontario. They knew he deserved the honour, because he'd had an outstanding career with plenty of recognition for his talents. They also realized that the 1980 drug charge could have tipped the scale against him, as far as the baseball writers were concerned. The fans may have forgiven him; after all some sports stars had been involved in far more nefarious activities. But the sports journalists clearly weren't ready to forgive Fergie yet.

There was a lot of controversy about this at the time of Fergie's induction. To maintain the honour's integrity, the BBWAA wanted its candidates to be absolutely lily white. Fergie's drug charge was a black mark against him, just as Gaylord Perry's skill with the illegal spitball was against him. The spitball and its variations are forbidden in baseball. This was one pitfall Jenkins never stepped into. A spitball is created when a pitcher applies a substance to the ball to make it heavier on one side, thus changing its dynamics as it travels through the air. Pitchers have been known to use saliva, vaseline or other substances concealed behind the ear or on the bill of a cap. Sometimes, pitchers have modified balls with sandpaper or a nail to give them an advantage. Before major leagues banned the spitball in 1920, this was a common practice.

It was feared that allowing offenders like Jenkins and Perry into the Hall of Fame would open the door for the admission of Pete Rose. Rose, an outstanding ball player, served a five-month prison term for tax felonies and had been banned from baseball in August, 1989 for gambling. He was one of 15 ball players who, over the years, had been banned for life from baseball for gambling.

Feelings ran high at the time of voting. A 13-man committee was set up to consider the rules of eligibility for the Hall of Fame. Some Hall of Fame inductees said that in the future they would boycott induction ceremonies if Rose were allowed in. Others, like Jenkins, felt that a ballplayer should be judged on his performance in baseball and on nothing else.

Gene Dziadura with his protégé's Plaque in Fergie Jenkins Field, Rotary Park in Chatham.

After Fergie ran fourth in the 1990 voting, the hometown fans

Gene Dziadura stands proudly beside Fergie Jenkins Field at Rotary Park in Chatham

began to get excited. They felt sure that 1991 would see their local hero enshrined in the Hall of Fame. After all, there was no other eligible candidate who could top his record. And it happened.

In 1991, 443 members of the BBWAA were eligible to vote. To be inducted into the Hall of Fame, a candidate would require 75% of the votes, or a total of 333. This time, Jenkins was the winner, with 334 votes, one more than the required number. No other player had entered the Hall of Fame with such a slim margin since Ralph Kiner slid through the door with 75.4%. Nevertheless, the city of Chatham went wild with joy.

Also scheduled to be inducted at the same time where Rod Carew who drew 401 votes, and Gaylord Perry who was redeemed with 342 votes.

Fergie got the good news at home in Guthrie, Oklahoma. Jack Lang, executive secretary of the BBWAA had phoned earlier and told Fergie to be at home at 5 p.m. when the results of the voting would be available. At five o'clock, Fergie was sitting by the telephone in a state of trepidation. It seemed like forever until at last the phone rang. It was Lang. He said "Let me be the first to congratulate you!" As soon as he hung up the phone, Fergie called his father to give him the good news. Next on his list of phone calls was Mike Bennett, sports editor of the *Chatham Daily News*. He called Bennett from the Dallas airport to make sure that he was among the first in the media to have the news story.

Shortly after, when Fergie was flying to New York, the TWA pilot made an announcement on the intercom.

"We'd like to extend a special TWA welcome to Ferguson Jenkins who is travelling with us tonight - he's been elected to baseball's Hall of Fame." The applause was enthusiastic. Fergie

Pitching at Chatham's Hall of Fame celebration in 1991

was asked to sign the flight attendant's passport which included autographs of such "greats" as Dustin Hoffman and Andre The Giant. The pilot offered Fergie a seat in first class, but with typical humility, the new Hall of Famer elected to remain in coach class.

Even before the official ceremony, the city of Chatham was

celebrating. Dominion Day, July 1st, 1991 was designated as Fergie Jenkins Recognition Day. Jenkins arrived at Rotary Park at 11.30 a.m. Gene Dziadura had persuaded him to put on his Cubs uniform. Fergie didn't think it was necessary, just to sign autographs, but he complied. What he didn't know was that many of his local baseball friends were hiding in the dugouts at Rotary Park, waiting to play ball with him. When Fergie was taken to the dugouts, there was a grand, tearful reunion with many old friends whom he hadn't seen for years. Among them was Jack Howe, the Bantam League pitcher whose sore arm had given Fergie his first chance to pitch in a game.

At 12.15 the City of Chatham made a presentation to Fergie. An Old Timers baseball game was on the schedule for 1 p.m., with Fergie's former minor baseball teammates on the diamond. The guest of honour threw out the first ball. Also playing were numerous winners of the Fergie Jenkins Award for the Chatham Minor Baseball Association's Player of the Year. Of course Fergie himself got into the game for a few innings, to the delight of the other players and the large crowd of spectators. Later, Fergie was grand marshal of a Parade of Nations through city streets.

At the end of the day, more than 5000 people crowded Tecumseh Park to watch Fergie receive honours from the City of Chatham, the County of Kent, the Township of Harwich, the Kinsmen Club, and the Chatham Minor Baseball Association. The latter group at that time announced the establishment of a Fergie Jenkins scholarship. Long after the scheduled events were over, Fergie stayed at the park chatting with fans and friends.

A further tribute came from the cultural side of the city as Chatham Museum featured a "Tribute to Fergie" exhibit daily, with free admission. Fans were delighted to see the display of photos, articles, trophies, baseballs, and other Jenkins memorabilia, including his Illinois licence plate with the identifying "FJ31". There was no doubt about it: Ferguson Jenkins Jr. was a popular sports hero to the people of Chatham.

As a permanent tribute to the city's most famous native, the entrance to town has a huge sign telling the whole world that

Chatham is "Home of Ferguson Jenkins". The sign was erected originally in 1971 as a tribute to Fergie. After his induction into the Hall of Fame, the sign was redesigned, and the words 'Baseball's Hall of Famer" were added.

Shortly before the big weekend in Cooperstown, Fergie was in Toronto for the Coca-Cola All-Star Fest, a big event held at the Convention Centre. It was a five-day event featuring such sports celebrities as Reggie Jackson, Johnny Bench, Rusty Staub - and of course, Ferguson Jenkins. On the final day, Fergie was at the Sky-Dome for the Heroes of Baseball Old Timers game. A crowd of 44,000 watched the American League team take on its National League counterpart. When Fergie was introduced at a pre-game ceremony, the standing ovation lasted a full minute. Before the game began, he was besieged by fans clamouring for autographs. Wearing his familiar Chicago Cubs uniform, Fergie pitched the first inning for the Nationals. He gave up one hit, and got three ground-ball outs. The Nationals won the game. Later that night, in white shirt and tie, Jenkins threw out the ceremonial first pitch for the major league all-star game that capped the day's festivities.

Hall of Fame weekend held three weeks later at Cooperstown also included a full schedule of events. There were golf and tennis tournaments, autograph sessions, buffet luncheons, dinners, receptions, a tour of the Hall of Fame, a group photo session, a press conference, even a Catholic Mass.

The induction ceremony itself was held at 2.30 p.m. on Sunday, July 21st on the lawn at the Hall of Fame Library. This was a special year for the Hall of Fame, for it was the first year when players from three different countries were inducted. The entire grounds was a sea of waving flags. In addition to the red maple leaf flown for Fergie, there were dozens of flags flying in honour of Rod Carew from Panama, and Gaylord Perry of the U.S.A.

For Ferguson Jenkins Jr. it was the pinnacle of success, the golden apple, the ring on the merry-go-round. In his acceptance of the bronze plaque showing himself in a Chicago Cubs cap, he spoke glowingly of all those who had helped him to achieve success in his chosen field. He thanked first his mother and his father; the people of Chatham; the fans in the cities where he played - Philadelphia, Boston, Arlington, Texas, Chicago; Tony Lucadello, head scout of the Phillies; his mentor Gene Dziadura and his family; and the boyhood friends who had maintained their connection and support for him throughout his career. He spoke warmly of Kathy, then of Mary Anne, his friend Cindy, and all of his children.

Fergie paid a special tribute to his father, saying "This day also belongs to my father. He was my first teacher. He inspired me, he taught me to be conscientious and responsible. On this day, I'm not being inducted alone. I'm being inducted on July 21 with Ferguson Jenkins Sr." Fergie Sr. was teary-eyed when he later told reporters, "This is the proudest day of my life."

Every visitor to Chatham knows that the city is the hometown of Fergie Jenkins, Hall of Fame member.

Young Fergie's thanks to his old friends at home were not misplaced, either. Chatham showed its support for Fergie Jenkins in spades. Between 200 and 300 people drove down for the occasion. Five busloads of people from Chatham and Kent County also went to see their hero receive his honour at Cooperstown. Two busloads were made up of players from the Chatham Minor Baseball Association and their parents. This was a once-in-a-lifetime opportunity for young ball players. The bus trip was paid for by Tom Reid, a Chatham native and an avid baseball fan. The group left Chatham before dawn on July 21st, reached Cooperstown in time for the ceremony in the afternoon, then promptly got on the bus again for the eight-hour return trip home. Another busload of fans enjoyed a tour organized by Homer Dick Travel for fans from the Chatham area, but fans from other parts of the province were in the crowd, too. Not all the fans were from Chatham and Kent Country, however. Canadians came to Cooperstown that day from other places such as Burlington and Simcoe.

Throughout the ceremony, Canadian flags were very much in evidence, for Fergie was the first (and still only) Canadian ever inducted into the Cooperstown Hall of Fame. During his speech, Fergie spoke with pride of being a Canadian. Throughout his career, he has always let it be known that he is Canadian through and through. It was certainly appropriate that the Chatham Concert Band entertained the crowd of more than 5,000 at the Hall of Fame induction ceremony. When bandleader Vaughn Pugh learned that Jenkins was being inducted, he got in touch with the Hall of Fame and offered his band's services. They agreed to include the band in their program, although they had never had a band at previous inductions. As Jenkins stepped out to the podium to accept his plaque, the Chatham Concert Band played "Canadian Sunset", the melody so often played on baseball fields across the U.S.A. when Fergie stepped up to bat.

As far as Fergie Jenkins was concerned, however, the most important fans in the crowd were his family. His father, Ferguson Sr. was there. He'd been saving his tuxedo for an important occasion like this, but when July 21st came, the temperature was 35°C, so hot that he had to give in and leave it behind in his hotel room. It was perhaps just as well; he would have burst the buttons off the jacket. He was so proud of his son. It was a tremendous thrill to see his son in front of that huge crowd, receiving baseball's highest honour in front of hundreds of fans, not to mention 31 Hall of Fame members, including Ted Williams, Joe DiMaggio and Willie Mays.

Other members of the family attended this special occasion, too. Daughters Kimberly, Dolores, Kelly and Samantha were

The Hall of Fame plaque

there, as well as Fergie's stepson Raymond, and his friend and later fiance, Cindy Takkiedine.

It was a proud day for Fergie and all who knew him. It was a proud day for Canada, too, as Ferguson Jenkins Jr. was the first Canadian to be inducted into the Baseball Hall of Fame.

The Baseball Hall of Fame at Cooperstown was dedicated on June 12th, 1939. That year was believed to be the 100th anniversary of baseball's beginning, and the site chosen for the Hall of Fame was just a block away from the late Elihu Phinney's former cow pasture where baseball was said to have been played a whole century before. Since then, sports historians have been discussing whether or not the legend of baseball's beginning is fact or fiction. It seems clear that the game of baseball evolved over centuries, having its roots in bat-and-ball games played in a number of different countries.

The first election to the Hall of Fame had been made in 1936 when the decision to establish this institution had been made. At that time, Ty Cobb, Babe Ruth, Honus Wagner, Christy Mathewson and Walter Johnson were officially inducted.

Fergie Jenkins was enshrined with the cream of the crop from the baseball world. To this day, he is still the only Canadian with a place of honour at Cooperstown.

18. More Honours To Come

When a baseball player has been chosen four times as Canada's outstanding male athlete, other honours don't come as surprises. Ferguson Jenkins won the Canadian Press poll of sportswriters and broadcasters in 1967, 1968, 1971 and 1972. This is a prestigious award for Canadian athletes, and Fergie's record topped that of the great Maurice "Rocket" Richard who won the honour three times.

The first time Fergie won the Canadian Male Athlete of the Year award, he outpolled hockey star Bobby Hull of the Chicago Black Hawks. Fergie could hardly believe it. "I beat Bobby?" he asked, when told of the award. "That's amazing. I knew I was in the running, but I didn't think I had a chance." Fergie was especially grateful that Canadian sports reporters from across the country had chosen him, since he was earning his living in Chicago, rather than a Canadian city. Of course, the same held true for Bobby Hull as well. Fergie had accumulated 276 points in the voting system, compared to Hull's 241.

In addition, he won the Lou Marsh Trophy in 1974. This annual award is named in honour of Lou Marsh, Canadian journalist and all around sportsman. Marsh, born in 1879, played with the Toronto Senior Argonaut football team, was a good sprinter and swimmer, and a racer of speedboats and iceboats. He was also a noted hockey and boxing referee. From 1925 until his death in 1936, Marsh wrote a daily sports column for the *Toronto Star*. It was called "With Pick and Shovel", indicating his determination in writing in-depth stories of the sports world.

The Lou Marsh Trophy is made of black marble, and stands about 75cm high. It is engraved with the winners' names, and is on display at the Canadian Sports Hall of Fame in Calgary.

Fergie's trophy was presented by Harry "Red" Foster, chairman of the selection committee at Jarry Park in Montreal. The event took place before a game between the Montreal Expos and the San Diego Padres, and was broadcast on national television. A crowd of 12,500 gave Fergie a standing ovation.

In his acceptance speech, Fergie said "Having looked over the list of previous winners, I am proud and honoured to be one of the individuals to receive this trophy."

To this day, Fergie Jenkins feels great pride in having his name engraved with such Canadian sports "greats" at Petra Burka, Marilyn Bell, Russ Jackson, Terry Fox, Wayne Gretzky, Jacques Villeneuve and Donovan Bailey. Fergie was the first baseball player to win the Lou Marsh Trophy since the award began in 1936.

All of these accolades earned Jenkins a new form of adulation. In the 1970s, the National Film Board produced a documentary about his career entitled *King of the Hill.* For months, a film crew followed him around from city to city, filming footage to show that a black Canadian could succeed in a big-time American sport.

In 1987, the Canadian sports hierarchy recognized Ferguson Jenkins once again. In that year, he made a trip to Calgary to accept membership in the Canadian Sports Hall of Fame. Honoured along with him were such Canadian sports "greats" as skier Steve Podborski; swimmer Alex Baumann; diver Sylvie Bernier; football stars Jackie Parker and Fritz Hanson: Jim Worrall of the International Olympic Committee, and Harold Wright who was president of the Canadian Olympic Association from 1969-77.

After Ferguson Jenkins was inducted into the Canadian Baseball Hall of Fame, then the Baseball Hall of Fame at Cooperstown, you might think that there was no other honour remaining. That was not the case.

Still more was in store. In March of 1992, Jenkins was summoned to the Cobo Hall's Riverfront Ballroom in Detroit to become a new member of the International Afro-American Sports Hall of Fame and Gallery.

That night, 12 outstanding athletes were inducted into the IAASHF. Two of them were Canadians, the first Canucks ever to be selected for this honour. In addition to Ferguson Jenkins, the other Canadian honoree was George "Kirky" Scott of Windsor. Scott was a former junior and senior hockey player, and at the time of the induction was a director of the Ontario Hockey

League and a boxing coach.

The germ of the idea for the IAASHF was planted in 1977 when Elmer Anderson asked Art Finney to write articles about former black athletes. So much material was collected that it became evident that a place was needed to house it. Furthermore, the history of blacks in sports was rapidly disappearing, and needed to be preserved in a safe place. In 1982, Anderson and Finney met with five other people to discuss the establishment of a Hall of Fame for this purpose in Detroit. The first three athletes were inducted in 1986. They were Joe Louis, Will Robinson and Richard "Night Train" Lane. Since then, 18 more stars had joined them including Sugar Ray Robinson, Muhammad Ali and Wilma Rudolph. Ferguson Jenkins was once again in elite company.

Induction into this celebration of Afro-American heritage did not win a fraction of the attention that the Cooperstown Hall of Fame recognition brought. Nevertheless, it was another indication of how highly Ferguson Jenkins is regarded by a wide spectrum of North Americans.

When the Ontario Sports Legends Hall of Fame was established at Pickering, Ferguson Jenkins Jr. was one of the 24 inaugural inductees. Candidates were chosen in 1995 and 1996, but were not inducted until the inaugural induction dinner took place on June 25th, 1997. The very first sports legend to be inducted was a horse called Big Ben, the greatest Canadian show jumper of all time. Fergie was also one of the 12 candidates chosen as an Ontario sports legend in the Hall of Fame's first year.

In baseball, the Triple Crown is not an official award. It's the unofficial opinion of an avid sports fan and stats wizard named Robert Minteer. He has calculated points and percentages based on Games Played; Innings Pitched; Games Won; Games Lost; Winning Percentages; Bases on Balls or Walks; Strikeouts; and Earned Run Averages. From this, he has compiled a list of 292 top pitchers going all the way back to 1876. In his book, Pitching's Triple Crown Contenders, Minteer refers to Fergie as "about as close to being a pure 'power pitcher' as they come."

On Minteer's scale, Fergie Jenkins rates 41st with a total of

143.86 points, compared to Walter Johnson's 387 points earned back in 1908 with the Washington team, and John Denny's 40 points amassed with St. Louis in 1976 and Cleveland in 1981. By the same method of rating, Fergie and Juan Marichal were just half a point behind Tom Seaver in 1969. On two other occasions, Fergie was a runner up before becoming a true TTC with 20.5 points in 1974 when he was with the Rangers.

The Canadian Baseball Hall of Fame and Museum, St. Marys, Ontario

19. Canadian Baseball Hall of Fame and Museum

Many baseball fans believe that the game of baseball originated in the U.S.A. Not true. For centuries, the people of Britain played a popular game called rounders, so-named because the players hit a ball with a club (as they called it) and ran around bases laid out in a diamond shape. There were other bat and ball games, too, with a great variety of regulations, and names such as trapball, stoolball and cat. The upperclass game of cricket evolved from these early games. So did baseball. When settlers came to North America - both Canada and the U.S.A. - they brought along rounders which eventually became known as base ball. No one person invented the game, and no one country can claim to be its original home.

For more than a century, however, it has been assumed that baseball began in the U.S.A. According to the National Baseball Hall of Fame at Cooperstown, New York, the rules for the game of baseball were devised by Abner Doubleday of Cooperstown in 1839.

Although many lifelong baseball fans don't realize it, the game goes back even farther than that in Canada. Adam Ford, a medical doctor who fled to Denver after being accused of poisoning a temperance leader, recorded the events surrounding a game played at Beachville, Ontario in 1838. The event was held on June 4th of that year at a celebration of the birthday of King George III which happened to coincide with another occasion for celebration, the end of the Rebellion of 1837. Ford, who attended the game as a child of seven, later wrote an account which appeared in the May 5th, 1886 edition of *The Sporting Life*, a Philadelphia publication.

The match, Ford wrote, was played between the Beachville Club and a team from the nearby townships of Zorra and North Oxford. It was obviously not the first game for either team. They used a ball made of woolen yarn, covered by calfskin sewn by the local shoemaker. The bat, which at that time was called the club, was made of cedar, Ford wrote, although at other times a wagon spoke or "any nice straight stick" would serve the purpose. The infield was a square, with five bases and baselines 24 yards apart. Ford was able to recall that there were fair and foul balls. At that time, he added, there were between six and nine innings, and anywhere from seven to twelve players per team, depending on who turned up.

In spite of the intervening years, Ford was even able to name some of the players. If Ford's description is accurate, it must have been based, at least in part, on accounts which he later heard from adults. It certainly would have been a much-discussed local event. There is no doubt that the game took place at the time and place described by Ford.

The game played on that occasion closely resembled the present game of baseball. Bob Barney, a London sports historian and professor at the University of Western Ontario, researched the event in depth and concluded that this was Canada's first organized baseball game.

As time went by, southwestern Ontario adopted the game as its own, with notable teams springing up in Windsor, Ingersoll, Woodstock, St. Thomas, London, Guelph, Petrolia and Chatham. Enthusiasm for the sport gradually spread throughout the rest of Canada. It may amaze many to learn that in 1876 - 8, the London Tecumsehs were the first professional baseball team, and one of the best in North America. They were invited to join the National League, but turned down the offer because League regulations would have prevented them playing lucrative local games with teams outside the league. It was 90 years before another Canadian team - the Montreal Expos - was invited into the big leagues.

In the early days, Canadians played a big part in major league baseball. In 1871, Mike Brannock of Guelph was the first Canadian to make it to the majors. He played with Chicago of the National Association in the 1871 and 1875 seasons.

Art Irwin of Toronto was not only a major league shortstop, but also a National League umpire in 1902, and a manager for eight seasons. Irwin, known as Doc or Cutrate or Sandy, is said to be the inventor of the fielders' glove. After he broke two fingers catching a ball bare-handed, he bought an extra large buckskin glove and stuffed it with padding. Voila! The fielders' glove was born. A few years after Irwin's debut in the majors, his younger brother John followed in his footsteps, playing in the National, American Association, Union and Players' Leagues.

In 1983, the Canadian Baseball Hall of Fame and Museum was incorporated as a non-profit charitable foundation dedicated to preserving Canada's baseball heritage. The original Canadian Baseball Hall of Fame shared space with the Hockey Hall of Fame at Exhibition Park in Toronto. When the Hockey Hall of Fame moved to Ontario Place, the baseball display was dismantled and put in storage in a Brampton warehouse. In 1992, it was decided that the Baseball Hall of Fame deserved a permanent home of its own, and proposals were invited from Ontario municipalities. A number of communities made submissions offering a permanent site for the Hall of Fame and Museum.

The attractive proposal offered by St. Marys was finally chosen. Because of its location in southwestern Ontario, not far from the site of the famous Beachville game, St. Marys was an appropriate location for the museum. The collection was moved from Brampton to the basement of the police station in St. Marys. Volunteers worked for months unpacking and sorting through the collection, a job made more difficult by the fact that labels had been removed from items and stored together in a separate box. Meanwhile, other volunteers worked 12-hour days preparing a place for the collection to be displayed.

St. Marys Cement Company donated 32 acres of land which now includes a new ball diamond, named in honour of Ferguson Jenkins, and the Museum and Hall of Fame located in an old, renovated building. In time, the collection will be moved to a large new building adjacent to the present site.

Since its establishment, the Canadian Baseball Hall of Fame and Museum has inducted 46 members. One of the earliest of these was Ferguson Jenkins Jr. who became a member in 1987.

In order to be eligible for induction, candidates must have been retired for five years, and have made a significant contribution to baseball in Canada. Most are ball players, but a few are coaches and administrators who made an impact on the game. Many items in the Museum collection, including those in the Ferguson Jenkins display, have been donated by the inductees. Every year, Fergie returns to the Canadian Baseball Hall of Fame for the induction of new members.

20. The Walk of Fame

Back in 1997, three Toronto friends sat discussing Canada's lack of a Walk of Fame, similar to the one in Hollywood. Diane Schwalm, Peter Soumalias and Bill Ballard batted the idea around, and decided to work toward establishing a Canadian Walk of Fame. As the result of persistence and hard work, they finally succeeded in having 13 blocks of streets in the theatre district of Toronto designated for their project. The streets wind past Festival Hall, the Princess of Wales and Royal Alexandra theatres, Roy Thompson Hall and CBC headquarters.

The first 14 Canadian celebrities to be inducted into the Walk were selected for the inaugural ceremony on June 25th, 1998. Since then, 51 famous Canadians or groups of Canadians have had stars embedded in the sidewalks in their honour. Induction in the Canadian Walk of Fame is a true honour, because unlike the Hollywood Walk of Fame where inductees are charged $1500 for their participation, this one has no strings attached.

The selected Walk of Fame celebrities for 2001 were announced at a press conference in Toronto on February 19th. The next morning, John Oddi read about it in the *Hamilton Spectator* when his wife, Mona, drew his attention to the article. They were delighted to learn that Fergie Jenkins was one of the nominees. In his role with the Fergie Jenkins Foundation, Oddi had recently been in touch with Fergie regarding the spring golf tournament. He immediately called Fergie at home, and discovered that he was breaking the news to the Jenkins household. Fergie was thrilled to know that he had been chosen for the list of inductees for the new millennium.

The list for 2001, he soon learned, included a diverse group of Canadians. They were hockey player Jean Beliveau, figure skater Kurt Browning, the late sprinter Harry Jerome, Inuit artist Kenojouak Ashevak, novelist Margaret Atwood, rock band The Guess Who, filmmaker Robert Lepage, actor Leslie Nielsen, polka king Walter Ostanek, director Ivan Reitman, opera singer Teresa Stratus, ballerina Veronica Tennant and, of course, Ferguson

Jenkins. This Millennium group joined outstanding Canadians from all fields of endeavour. The Canadian Walk of Fame includes internationally known Canadian celebrities such as Gordie Howe, Martin Short, William Shatner, Donald Sutherland, Michael J. Fox and many others. With his fellow nominees for 2001, Ferguson Jenkins brought the total number of inductees to 51.

John Oddi noticed in the newspaper article about Fergie's nomination that Jenkins was the only celebrity whose travel plans had not been finalized. He quickly got in touch with Carl Kovacs, and soon found himself appointed by the Foundation as liaison person for the Walk of Fame event. His first step was to make arrangements for Fergie and his party to attend the event in June. Travel arrangements and hotel accommodation needed to be taken care of. Plane tickets were arranged for Fergie and Lydia who stayed at the posh Four Seasons Hotel in Toronto, while Fergie's daughter Kimberley, her friend and Marie and Gene Dziadura checked in at the Holiday Inn in Oakville. Land transportation had to be arranged for everyone to get to and from the special events. Next on Oddi's list was to make sure Fergie selected and approved the form in which he wanted his name to appear in the inscription on the Walk of Fame star. Fergie chose "Ferguson Arthur Jenkins." He also chose Gene Dziadura as his guest presenter.

It was a very exciting time for them all, for it meant dressing "to the nines" for one of the biggest honours in Canada.

Meanwhile, John Oddi was working behind the scenes to obtain complimentary tickets for the entire party, including those in the Foundation who had worked hard at co-ordinating Fergie's itinerary. He requested tickets for sixteen people. Peter Soumailis commented "You ordered more tickets than The Guess Who!" Oddi later learned that a special executive meeting had to be held to approve this unusual number of tickets for the Jenkins party.

The official ceremony took place in pouring rain outside Roy Thompson Hall on Friday, June 1st. All the celebrities with their parties socialized indoors over drinks and hors d'oeuvres until moment arrived. One by one, the celebrities and their guests were taken to their stars for the official unveilings. Terry Gilloch, Fergie's celebrity assistant for the day, came to get the Jenkins party when his turn came. They were taken by limo to Fergie's star on Simcoe Street. There, with a flourish, Jenkins whipped away a banner to reveal his star to the public for the very first time.

When all the stars had been unveiled, everyone was seated in the main Roy Thompson Hall theatre for the presentation of the Walk of Fame star trophies to the inductees. When it was time for Ferguson Jenkins to accept his trophy, he was introduced to the audience by his long-time friend and mentor, Gene Dziadura. In his speech, Dziadura pointed out Fergie's outstanding record of 284 wins; seven 20-win seasons, six of them in succession; more than 3000 strikeouts and less than 1000 walks in 19 years of major league pitching.

The audience had just been watching scenes from Fergie's life shown on a large screen, and the views of his mother and father made a tear slip down his

Fergie and his presenter, Gene Dziadura with the Walk of Fame star. You can hardly notice the bent point on the star.

cheek. Visibily shaken, he grabbed Lydia for support. She came and stood close beside him at the podium. After accepting the award, he took off his glasses to wipe the tear away, and momentarily took his hand off the 30-lb. trophy which was on the podium. It fell on the floor, barely missing Lydia's foot.

"Good thing I wasn't a shortstop," Fergie quipped to the crowd who cheered and clapped. Later, Fergie pointed out to friends that his trophy was not *exactly* like all the others because one point of the star was slightly bent!

During his acceptance speech, Fergie pointed out Gene and Marie Dziadura sitting in the audience. Fergie recounted once again the well-known story of hitting the wastebasket during one of his early training sessions with Dziadura.

Being chosen for the Walk of Fame is no small thing. To qualify, candidates must have been born in Canada or spent their formative/creative years in this country. They must have been successful for at least 10 years, and have a body of work recognized for its impact on our cultural heritage.

During September and October, the Walk of Fame's media sponsors solicit nominations from the public. Nominations come through the Walk of Fame website, by telephone, by fax and by mail. Then the candidates are chosen by the board of directors which reviews ballots submitted by the public. When the competition closed on December 31st, 2000, more than 40,000 ballots had been submitted by Canadians from coast to coast. Nominations for future years can be made at the website http://www.canadaswalkoffame.com

The *Chatham Daily News* proudly proclaimed the news of Fergie's induction into the Walk of Fame with the June 2nd headline on the sports page "Fergie gets a 'walk'."

On the Sunday after the induction into the Walk of Fame, Fergie threw out the first ball for the Blue Jays' home game against Boston at the Sky Dome, and gave colour commentaries on CBC television between innings. During the game, he and his family and friends were wined and dined in a private box at the Sky Dome. The weekend also included many interviews with the media, including a TSN taping with Michael Landsberg, a taping for the Mike Bullard Show, and a live phone interview with Humble and Howard, a radio sports show. Sandwiched into the weekend as well as a Foundation board of directors meeting in St. Catharines on Saturday. Serious business did not get lost in the middle of a weekend of fun and glamour

When leaving the hotel for the plane trip home, Fergie asked Carl Kovacs to drive him and Lydia to his star. This time, there was no traffic, so they all got out and Carl took snapshots of Lydia

Fergie kneels by his Walk of Fame star on Simcoe Street in Toronto

and Fergie kneeling by the star. It was a very moving moment for all of them. It showed, once again, that although Fergie takes everything in his stride, there is a very sensitive heart behind his calm exterior.

Next stop for Lydia and Fergie was the airport, but Lydia suddenly remembered that she had left some of her belongings in the hotel room, and wanted to go back for them. Fergie was sure that they would be gone by now, but Lydia insisted, so Carl took them back to the Four Seasons. Fergie sat in the van while Lydia and Carl went inside to retrieve her things. There was no problem, but it took a few minutes for them to be brought out of storage. After 20 minutes or so, Fergie strolled in to see what was taking so long. A moment later, a driver walked into the lobby and called out "Limousine for Fergie Jenkins!"

"Did you order a limousine?" Carl asked.

"No," Fergie replied, perplexed. It seems that it was part of the Walk of Fame service. So the Jenkins' luggage was transferred to the limousine for the trip to Pearson Airport. It turned out well, and in the process, several limousine drivers got autographed baseballs.

It was a very exciting time for Fergie, his family and his friends from the Foundation. It was a thrill for the whole party to be part of such a successful stellar event. Pulling it all together so that it worked smoothly was not only a tribute to the Walk of Fame administrators, but also to the Fergie Jenkins Foundation. The members of the Foundation Board of Directors were delighted to meet such famous Canadians as Jean Beliveau, Brian Linehan, Burton Cummings and Leslie Nielson. After all, the Directors are volunteers, ordinary Canadians who seldom have the opportunity to rub shoulders with the country's elite celebrities.

21. The Second Dream

Although he grew up in a small city - Chatham had a population of 35,000 in those days - Fergie was always attracted to country life. By 1971, he'd earned a solid reputation in big league baseball. His salary was $75,000, but he felt he was worth more. His first move was to attempt to negotiate with vice-president John Holland of the Cubs. That proved to be fruitless. He was offered $10,000.

Under the new Basic Agreement contract between players and clubs which had been signed the previous summer, it was permissible for a player to hire an attorney to help him with negotiations. This had never been done before, and the practice was frowned on, even though it was now acceptable. When Fergie could not make any progress on his own, he hired David Schiata, a Montreal lawyer, to negotiate on his behalf for $100,000 for the coming season. As happens with negotiations, he settled for less, but the final sum of $90,000 was satisfactory as far as Fergie was concerned. He had expected to sign for less than the amount he was asking for.

At the time, some people thought his demand a little unreasonable. Sports figures' salaries in those days were very modest compared to the 1990s when players demanded and received huge incomes. Still, Fergie's negotiations had uncovered the fact that the Cubs were making lots of money from gate receipts, television and radio contracts and other sources. The club was not really "hard up", and Fergie planned to continue to work hard for it.

So why did Jenkins go after this increase? The answer was simple. He felt that he'd shown his value out on the mound, and was entitled to additional monetary recognition. He was sometimes quoted as saying "The only difference between me and Bob Gibson is $60,000". Gibson, pitcher with the St. Louis Cardinals, also had five 20-win seasons to his credit, but he was earning $150,000. There was another difference between Jenkins and Gibson, however; Fergie had the Cy Young Award.

Now he wanted to fulfill his second big dream by buying a farm, near Blenheim in southwestern Ontario.

"I want to grow a little corn maybe. And raise dogs, too. I like dogs," he said at the time. There was an urgency in Fergie's desire to buy land because he felt strongly that within a few years, all the good agricultural land and woodlots in southwestern Ontario would be razed for development. If he was ever going to own land near his hometown, he'd have to buy it soon. It was part of his

On a visit to Canada, Fergie enjoyed fishing in one of his favourite spots

dream to keep part of the wooded area of his land as a game preserve.

The dream of owning a farm and operating a kennel where good hunting dogs could be raised and trained was not just "pie in the sky" for this athlete. It was something he really longed to do, and at last it was within his reach. After so many years of living in city apartments, he was looking forward to being able to spend time in a place where he could really stretch out, both physically and mentally.

In 1972, an outstanding season and the Cy Young Award earned Fergie a two-year contract for $125,000 each year. Now he could invest in the land he loved. There was also an opportunity to purchase a farm near Chicago, but Fergie decided that he wanted to stick close to his Canadian roots. He purchased a 100-acre farm near Blenheim in southwestern Ontario, and named it the Circle J. He had a house built on the property for himself, Kathy and their two daughters, Kelly and Delores. While Fergie was off to spring training in Florida, Kathy stayed behind to supervise the finishing touches on the house and do the

Fergie and friends on a hunting trip to Canada

decorating. In moving to Blenheim, Fergie reassured friends and fans in his hometown that, although he had to spend a good deal of time on other parts of the continent, he and Kathy still considered themselves to be Chathamites. The farm was barely ten miles from Fergie's hometown, but he wanted everyone to know that his heart was still in the city of his birth.

Dogs had been part of Fergie's second dream for a long time. He'd started hunting with a .22 at the age of 14, and discovered he loved it. He bought his first good dog in 1963. He was a German shorthaired pointer with a lot of promise.

"I started training him at six or seven months. When I left for spring training, he was just getting real birdy," Fergie recalls. "When I came back, he was spoiled. You know how kids are. They'd come around and pet him. And he drove around all summer with a friend, on the seat of his convertible." That first dog, through no fault of its own, was a disappointment. It seemed that without a dedicated trainer, a dog like that could easily be distracted from the serious business of hunting.

Soon this failure was in the past. By 1971, Fergie had five shorthaired pointers and eight English pointers, kept on a friend's farm near Petrolia. His first good dog came from Illinois, and was called Buckskin Sudden Sam. This gave Fergie a start at breeding shorthaired pointers. He made a special effort to produce light-coloured dogs which seemed to be in demand. The animals from the Circle J had brown heads and lighter bodies with spots. These dogs were much in demand in the U.S.A., but were not popular with Canadian hunters who seemed to prefer labs, beagles and shepherds.

The ranch grew until there were 30 dogs, plus the ones that Fergie boarded. By law, this required that the premises have cement floors, showers, a septic tank. The pups had to be needled, and a local veterinarian came regularly to inspect the premises. Fergie had thoughts about going to veterinary college if the baseball career didn't work out. Meanwhile, he took night courses in some aspects of veterinary training, and invested in dozens of books on subjects that would help him look after his animals better. He also took a welding course which proved to be an asset in repairing equipment around the farm.

As soon as the baseball season ended each year, he'd be back in Chatham. Every day he could, he'd pick up some of his dogs and head for Mitchell's Bay on Lake St. Clair for a day of duck hunting. Not all of his fans approved of his love of hunting. When members of the Audubon Society learned that he sometimes shot pigeons in Chicago to keep his dogs in shape, he received a flood of letters of protest. This was one issue on which he and his fans simply had to disagree. There was no chance that he would give up hunting.

Fergie wasn't just a dilettante when it came to hunting and fishing. He was a knowledgeable expert. He was invited to appear with Red Fisher on *Canadian Outdoors* in a segment on caribou hunting in Saskatchewan, and he did another television program on moose hunting in northeastern Ontario for CFTO-TV.

As an avid hunter, Fergie liked the shorthairs because they swim and will retrieve in the water. However, they didn't seem to be as popular with Canadians as other breeds, so in time, dog breeding gave way to raising cattle. The farm had Angus, Charolais and Limousin cattle. In addition to his own 100 acres, Fergie leased another 100 so that the venture was a real working farm with all the equipment that's required to run such an extensive operation.

Eventually, as his career took greater demands, the farm had to be sold. But Fergie was and still is a farmer at heart. As soon as the opportunity came along, he went back to rural life as the owner of Lakeview Ranch in Guthrie, Oklahoma.

Although his home is now at Lakeview Ranch, Fergie has never given up his Canadian citizenship. He is still looks forward to frequent family visits in Canada. These days, many of his personal appearances are also in Canada.

Fishing has been another lifelong passion with Jenkins. Over the years, he has taken every opportunity to return to southwestern Ontario to enjoy fishing with his friends. It's a love he learned from his father.

Fishing was often a family adventure for the Jenkins. Delores would sit in the car, sometimes knitting, while the two Fergies dropped a line in the water.

On one such occasion, when Fergie was about ten years old, he and his father were fishing off a pier in Lake Erie. Fergie Jr. was having trouble sitting still long enough to let the fish bite. In spite of his father's admonitions, he kept jumping around and accidentally backed off the pier. The water was deep there, and although he knew how to swim, the youngster was so frightened by the shock that every time he surfaced, he went down again. By lying on his stomach, Fergie Sr. was finally able to grasp the boy's hands and drag him out to safety. It was a tremendous fright for the whole family, but the next weekend, they were back again in the same spot, with strict orders for the youngest Jenkins to "Sit still!" The experience didn't sour young Fergie on fishing, or on swimming. He still loves both sports to this day. Love of fishing may be a generational inheritance from Fergie's paternal ancestors who fished in the Barbados.

22. Some Dreams Don't Last

One writer has described Fergie's life as something from "The Book of Job." Fergie doesn't look back on his own life in this way at all. While it's true that his baseball career was a series of successes, with only minor setbacks to create a little interest, his personal life by contrast has been a series of tragedies. In spite of the pain they've caused, Fergie remains a cheerful, out-going person without a bit of spite or anger.

First of all was his mother's blindness which was perhaps inevitable, but was hastened by the trauma of his birth. To the entire family, it was a sadness that Delores never really saw her son clearly, or saw him play baseball in front of a huge crowd of cheering fans. Although she followed his career closely, savouring every new achievement, delighting in every honour, she did not have the joy of actually seeing him on the mound. Whenever possible, Delores and Ferguson Sr. attended games, but always with a portable radio so that Delores could follow the play and join in the cheering.

Delores took up five-pin bowling and became winner of the trophy for high average in the Western Ontario Blind Bowlers Association. For several years, she was a respected member of the executive of the Canadian National Institute for the Blind.

From Fergie's earliest days in sports, Delores faithfully kept a scrapbook of newspaper and magazine articles about her son. Although she never read a word of them, she knew each one by heart and lovingly pasted it into the latest scrapbook.

It was a great sadness for the entire family, for everyone who knew her, when Delores died of stomach cancer in September, 1970. She was 54 years old. She had been the guiding light, the beacon of strength to all who knew her. The young men of the Adelaide Street Gang mourned her deeply. People all over Chatham missed her.

Before Delores died, Fergie took every opportunity to fly or drive home from Chicago to see her. Although she was delighted to have him at her bedside, she selflessly encouraged him to carry on with his own life. Shortly before she died, Fergie came to see her. As she held his hand, she urged

"You go back. You have to do what you do best. You have to live your life."

On the day she died, he was pitching against Pittsburgh. He hurried home as soon as he received the news, arriving there the same day. He was scheduled to pitch against St. Louis the following day. When he got home, his father said "Your mother would have wanted you to pitch", so Fergie called Durocher and told him he would come back. Durocher wisely replied "No. Stay with your family." The Cubs lost the game.

The day after his mother's funeral, Fergie was back on the mound, doing what he did best - pitching a ball. It had been a frustrating, tiring trip to Montreal where the Cubs were playing. Weary and heartsick, Fergie nevertheless pitched a good game, beating the Expos 3 - 2.

He had remembered what his mother had said to him once before when they'd talked about his concerns. She said "Get out there and do your best. You wouldn't be in a major league uniform if you didn't belong in one." He realized that she was right, and it would be a tribute to her for him to concentrate on the game and do his very best. He also knew that in future, he was going to miss having his mother to advise and support him in troubled times.

"I was tested when my mother was sick," Fergie recalled. "I had a tattoo put on my arm. It says 'Trust in God'. Some people questioned that, but it was a good thing for me. Every time I feel bad, I just look at my arm." One thing Fergie has regretted is that his mother did not live to know of the honours he has earned, the Cy Young Award, the Hall of Fame induction and all the rest.

"He really worshipped Delores," Gene Dziadura recalls. "He was her best friend. It was very hard for him when she died."

On February 13th, 1965, Fergie married Anne Katherine Williams of Dresden, a small town about 16 miles from Chatham. They had first met while they were in high school, although they did not attend the same school. Kathy went to the Ursuline College for girls. The couple actually met at a Young People's meeting at William Street Baptist church. The meetings were on Sunday evenings from seven until nine. Afterwards, some of the young people including Kathy and Fergie would go roller skating at the Kiwanis Arena. Kathy and Fergie frequently skated together, and they soon became known as a couple. They dated for six years before becoming engaged in 1963. Fergie proposed over the telephone, and sent the ring by mail.

Kathy is descended from Josiah Henson, the black slave who in 1830, escaped to Upper Canada with his wife and children. Once safely across the border, he set up a community at Dresden where other escaped slaves could make a new life. It is said that Josiah Henson was the model used by Harriet Beecher Stowe for Uncle Tom in *Uncle Tom's Cabin.* There are still many black families in southwestern Ontario, many of them like Kathy descended from Henson and his followers.

At their wedding, Kathy was given away by Thomas Henson, her mother's brother. The wedding took place at William Street Baptist Church in Chatham, the same church where the bride and groom had met. It was a large affair with about 200 guests. That evening, the bride and groom and some of their friends left the reception to drive out to the Community Centre where the Supremes were performing. They knew the Supremes, and wanted to say "Hello" before returning to the wedding reception. Afterwards, the newlyweds drove to Florida where Fergie was scheduled to begin spring training with the Phillies.

Life with the Big Leagues turned out to be very busy. Fergie was on the road or off playing winter ball. When he was at home in Chatham, he was working hard at training, plus looking after the farm and kennel.

Although Fergie and Kathy wanted children, they were slow in coming. In 1970, Kathy suffered a miscarriage, just when they thought their dream of having a family was about to come true. They finally made the decision to adopt, and Kelly Loren joined their household. Almost immediately, Kathy became pregnant so that before long, Kelly had a sister, Delores. Later, Kimberly became the "little sister" in the household. The couple hoped one day to have a son, but when Kathy had three more miscarriages, this dream was set aside.

During those busy years, Kathy and Fergie led a mostly quiet life. They were close friends with Billy Williams and his wife, Shirley, with whom they often socialized. Also close with Kathy and Fergie, as well as with Delores and Fergie Sr. were Dorothy and Arthur Zellar of Evanston, Illinois. The Zellars were closer to the senior Jenkins' in age, but had adopted Kathy and Fergie since their move to Chicago. The friendship began when Zellar, a regular at Wrigley Field, leaned over the railing to chat with Fergie in the bullpen. When Fergie was pitching at home, Arthur Zellar often phoned Delores after the game to give her a play-by-play account of the day. He also contributed many of the newspaper clippings that Delores carefully pasted into her scrapbooks. The whole family was devasted when Zellar died in his sleep of a heart attack.

The strain of Fergie's busy lifestyle, the constant travel, took its toll on the marriage. In 1984, Kathy and Fergie decided to separate. It wasn't a happy time. After more than 20 years of marriage, they were divorced in 1987. Over the years, the two have kept in touch, with the children as their common bond, but they are no longer close. Even after the divorce, Kathy continued to look in often on Ferguson Sr., taking his groceries to him and doing other errands. Gene Dziadura describes her as "ten feet tall", a very strong woman.

For a time, Fergie felt disenchanted with women, wasn't interested in dating at all. Then one day, Ray Meyer called and asked him to come to Chicago to go to a Bears' football game. After the game, the two went out for a drink. Also at the bar were members of a local women's softball team who quickly recognized Jenkins. One of those players was Mary-Anne Miller who took a dare from a friend and introduced herself to the baseball hero. They talked for a while, and discovered they had a lot in common.

The two began dating almost at once. Mary-Anne and her son, Raymond, came to Canada and spent some time in Blenheim, getting acquainted with Fergie's family and friends, and the city he called "Home". At this time, Kathy was still living at the Circle J. Fergie, Mary-Anne and Raymond then went to Chicago where Fergie was working at the time.

In 1988, Fergie and Mary-Anne were married at one of the wedding chapels in Las Vegas. Brad Fisher, Fergie's close friend from Chatham, was the best man.

That same year Fergie and Mary-Anne bought a 160-acre ranch near Guthrie, Oklahoma. Fergie had accepted a minor league coaching job with the Texas Rangers' AAA team in Oklahoma City. The newlyweds felt it was the ideal time to make a new start. Fergie sold his farm near Chatham, and they began looking for the perfect home near Oklahoma City. When the real estate agent took them to see the spread near Guthrie, Mary-Anne looked at the expanse, the two artificial lakes from a rise in the ground and said "I like this. I like it here." That settled the matter. The deal was signed, and the place was named Lakeview Ranch.

The coaching job didn't last long, but that was fine because the ranch required a lot of repairs and maintenance. Then there

were the cattle and the Appaloosa horses to be cared for. It was a great deal of work, but both Fergie and Mary-Anne loved it. There was a small house on the ranch. They renovated it and enlarged it into a comfortable 8,000-square foot home. Mary-Anne brought her son, Raymond from a previous marriage into the

Mary-Anne and Fergie tie the knot in Las Vegas. - Jenkins family photo

family, and Fergie gladly adopted the boy. Soon, their family grew with the addition of a little girl, Samantha who brought new sunshine to Lakeview Ranch.

In December, 1991, Mary-Anne was driving home from work as finance officer for an auto dealership. It was about a 30-minute drive from the office in Oklahoma City to Lakeview Ranch. Somewhere along the road, something went terribly wrong. Mary-Anne was an excellent driver, but the rear tire of her vehicle blew out, and she lost control of her car. It rolled over three times. For some reason, she wasn't wearing her seat belt, a most unusual oversight for her. She was thrown through the windshield. She suffered a broken neck, broken clavicle, two punctured ribs and a punctured lung.

Fergie was in Arizona when a call came through to tell him about the accident. He rushed back home to be at her bedside. Although her injuries were serious, they were not expected to be life-threatening. She was unable to speak, but after a few days, she seemed to be improving. Then, about three weeks later, while Fergie was away, she developed pneumonia.

Fergie learned about this new development when he arrived back from a press conference following the announcement of his forth-coming induction into the Baseball Hall of Fame in Cooperstown, New York. He hurried to Mary-Anne's bedside with a sheaf of newspaper clippings about the event.

Raymond and Mary-Anne at Church - Jenkins family photo

When he first went in to see her, she was very tired and couldn't stay awake. The next morning, he returned to read the clippings to her. Mary-Anne sat up in bed, and still unable to speak, smiled happily in appreciation of the praise being heaped on her husband.

Now that Mary-Anne seemed to be improving, Fergie felt it was safe to attend another scheduled press conference in New York. While he was gone, Mary-Anne's condition worsened, and she quietly passed away. Although Fergie hurried back once again, it was too late.

This was a traumatic time for Fergie, Raymond and Samantha. Mary-Anne, just 32 years old, was buried near Lakeview Ranch, the place she loved so much. She never did see the completion of the new house that was being built on the farm. Fergie settled in to life as a single parent, learning to be both mother and father to his children. It turned out to be a full-time job. Both children required a lot of attention. Samantha was still a toddler. Raymond was entering his teens, a critical time in any youngster's life. He was playing ball with the local Little League team. Although he was not one of the best players on the team, he was holding his own, but needed plenty of support and encouragement. Fergie was there for him all the way. Still, it was tough for the youngster to be the son of a Hall of Fame baseball player, yet unable to hit the ball consistently. With his hands full at home, Fergie couldn't think of going back to coaching at that time.

On top of it all, Fergie had many questions that kept turning over in his mind. Why was Mary-Anne speeding on that road, when she usually was a very careful driver and seldom went over the speed limit? Why didn't she have her seatbelt on? Was another vehicle involved in some way? Had she swerved to avoid an animal or a person on the road? They were questions that could no longer be answered, yet they rankled just the same. The uncertainty prolonged the healing period. But Fate wasn't through with Ferguson Jenkins Jr. yet.

In Guthrie, Oklahoma, Fergie enjoyed a quiet time with Samantha and Raymond

After Mary-Anne's death, a friend from the past appeared on the scene and offered to help look after the house and children. She was Cindy Takieddine whom Fergie had met in 1967 when he was playing with the Chicago Cubs. He was 23 at the time, and Cindy was 17, the daughter of an Air Force officer stationed in Phoenix. They had been friends at that time, and stayed in touch from time to time, but hadn't seen each other in about 15 years.

Like Fergie, Cindy eventually married. In 1983, her husband went back to the Middle East on a family errand and was not heard from again. Eventually, Cindy filed for divorce on the grounds of abandonment. For nearly 20 years, she worked in the fashion industry before deciding to study for a serious career in law. She was working in a Los Angeles law office when a friend told her about Fergie's induction into the Hall of Fame, and the death of his wife. She called the Chicago Cubs' office and asked if they would forward a letter of combined congratulation and condolence to Fergie. They agreed to do so. When Fergie read the letter, he called Cindy who was impressed by his plight - from career father to stay-at-home Dad with a 23-month old daughter and a 12-year-old son.

Cindy and a friend were about to go on vacation, so Cindy suggested that they should come to Guthrie and help out a bit. Cindy's offer came just when Fergie needed it most. Samantha was at an active stage in her life, and Raymond was having a hard time dealing with the loss of his mother. Fergie really needed a break from his full-time job as Dad. Cindy and her friend cooked, cleaned and looked after the children, bringing a sense of normalcy to the Jenkins household. At the end of the vacation time, Cindy's friend went home, but Cindy stayed on.

Samantha had taken to Cindy at once, and immediately began calling her Mom. Mary-Anne was 5'11; Cindy was 5'10 so there was some similarity in their appearances. Things worked out well at first. Cindy and Samantha became very close. So did Cindy and Fergie. In fact, friends began to take it for granted that they would get married. In the spring of 1992, they became engaged but made no marriage plans. They talked about it, but it just didn't seem like a priority at the time. There was no need to rush.

As time went by, Fergie began to have some doubts. Cindy was a tremendous help in every way, yet she was showing some alarming signs of jealousy. Since his induction into the Hall of Fame, he was receiving huge amounts of fan mail. He read it all, and answered as much as he could. Cindy often would open mail for him. Sometimes, she would see that a letter was from a woman and would throw it away. Always conscientious about his fan mail, Fergie would be annoyed when he found a discarded letter. He told Cindy that the letters were his, and were not to be treated like that. Sometimes angry words would ensue.

In the fall of 1992, Fergie was offered a job coaching young pitchers with the Cincinnati Reds' farm team in Chattanooga. For a retired professional ballplayer, it was a perfect job. For Fergie, it was an

Samantha Jenkins, age three - Jenkins family photo

answer to a silent prayer. In 1989 and 1990, Fergie had worked for the Texas Rangers' Triple A team as pitching coach. It was the job that had brought him and Mary-Anne to Oklahoma. But when Mary-Anne died in 1991, he just couldn't continue. His top priority at that time was to take care of Samantha and Raymond.

Nevertheless, Fergie itched to get back to baseball. It had been his life for so many years that it was hard to think of the future without baseball. So the offer from the Reds provided an opportunity to use his years of knowledge and skill to help up-and-coming talent in a sport that he loved. He was considering the job seriously, had even accepted it verbally, but hadn't yet signed a contract. He and Cindy talked several times about the job and their other problems. Although she seemed depressed, Fergie felt sure that everything would work out in the end.

The story about his acceptance of the job as pitching coach hit the sports pages on Tuesday, December 1st. As fate would have it, a reporter telephoned from Cincinnati to confirm the story and offer his congratulations to Fergie on getting this desirable job.

Cindy took the call. She was very upset when she realized that Fergie had accepted the job verbally without telling her that he had done so. Although Fergie clearly recalled discussing it with her several times and explaining how important the job was to him, she was angry and felt left out of the decision-making. She had been dreading the possibility that he would take the job, and that she would be left alone on the ranch for eight months at a stretch. Although she enjoyed farm life, she just didn't believe that she could handle the whole thing on her own. Realizing that this was now about to become a reality, she fell even more deeply into depression.

No one will ever know if it would have made any difference if Cindy and Fergie had had the opportunity to talk the situation out once again. Perhaps if she had understood how much the job meant to him, she might have been able to accept his great need to be out on the diamond. But the opportunity for more serious talk never came.

On December 15th - once again, just before Christmas, just after his birthday - Fergie was in Guthrie doing errands. He dropped by Samantha's day care centre and told a staff member that he would pick up Samantha at 5.30 because he thought Cindy was going Christmas shopping later in the day. He hadn't seen Samantha and Cindy since early that morning, and everything had seemed to be fine then.

Meanwhile, Cindy dressed Samantha in her pretty green party dress and shiny black shoes. She told Samantha that they were going to a Christmas party at the day care centre. But there was no party. Instead, Cindy drove her Bronco to a isolated road in the country about 30 miles from home, attached a vacuum hose from the car's exhaust pipe into the car, sealed the doors with tape, and held Samantha close on the back seat while the car idled. Carbon monoxide poisoning killed them both. An oil-field worker discovered the tragic site shortly afterwards, but too late to save their lives.

Back at the ranch, Fergie was working outside and was almost ready to leave to pick up Samantha when the sheriff's office called and said that Sheriff Doug Powell wanted to see him right away. Fergie was puzzled about the call, but jumped into his truck and drove to town immediately. When Sheriff Powell broke the news to him, Fergie didn't believe it at first. He explained that he was just about to pick up Samantha at the day care centre. He was sure she was there. To satisfy the frantic father, Powell called the day care, and was assured that Samantha had not been there at all that day. The Sheriff's deputy drove Fergie out to the site to identify the bodies, the saddest experience of his lifetime.

Cindy had left a note saying that she couldn't bear Fergie's betrayal - an obvious allusion to the job he had accepted. Her reason for taking Samantha with her was that she didn't want to leave her without a mother. The note, written on the back of a lumber company receipt, also said "Contact Ferguson Jenkins. He can claim the bodies."

The unpleasant task of breaking the news to Fergie's children fell to Kathy. Kelly, 22; Delores, 21; and Kimberly, 15 all headed for Guthrie as soon as their mother told them of the tragedy. Other years, they had come to the ranch to celebrate Christmas as a family. This year, they came to attend a double funeral. Ferguson Sr. was just not up to making the trip. He was in a nursing home, and felt he'd seen enough sadness in the family already. He grieved privately.

The funeral service was held a few days later at St. Mary's Catholic Church in Guthrie. Interment took place at Maple Leaf Cemetery, a small county burial place adjacent to Lakeview Ranch. Samantha was buried between her mother and Cindy.

The day after Christmas, Fergie had the unhappy task of returning Christmas gifts to local stores - clothing for Cindy, a Cabbage Patch doll and other little-girl toys for Samantha.

"I was so angry," Fergie says. "There were days when I was really angry. My uncle told me to burn down the farmhouse, because it was unlucky but I couldn't do it." He did get a priest to bless it, though, just in case. Friends worried about Fergie, for in spite of his easygoing manner, he was obviously experiencing intense, heartbreaking pain.

Morbid thoughts spun in his head in the middle of long, sleepless nights. Why did Cindy feel compelled to do it? Why hadn't they talked about their problems more? Would it have made a difference if they had been married? Were there any clues to her intentions that he should have noticed? Why did she take that lovable little girl with her when she knew how much Samantha meant to him? Who fell asleep first? Was it Samantha, or was she alone and frightened for a while? All the questions a bereaved parent asks after a tragedy like that beset the Hall of Famer.

Like others in similar situations, Fergie found comfort in a support group for parents who have lost children. Then there were hundreds of letters from fans and others who offered sympathy. Many letters told of other losses and tragedies that touched Fergie poignantly. Now, he could relate to those losses completely.

"I still get choked up when I see young girls," he says. "One time I missed a flight because I was crying too hard to take my ticket up to the attendant at the gate."

Fortunately, Ferguson Jenkins Jr. does not give up easily. Otherwise, he would never have reached the Big Leagues, never won the Cy Young Award, never made it into the Baseball Hall of Fame. One pastor reminded him that God never puts more pressure on a man than he can bear. The burdens bestowed on Fergie show that God knows His baseball hero is a man of exceptional strength.

These losses began a new stage in Fergie's life. Although it was an additional loss to him, Jenkins decided not to take the job as pitching coach after all. For several years, he had been hoping for just such a spot in the baseball world. It was something he could do well, a new career that would provide great satisfaction in helping young pitchers to excel.

But for Fergie, family still came first. Raymond was only 13 years old, on the brink of the teens, and in need of all the love and guidance that young people crave. Besides, Raymond was still grappling with the loss of his own mother, less than two years before. Fergie knew he could not abandon him to strangers while he left the ranch for months at a time. He made the decision to give his full attention to Raymond for as long as he needed it. So Fergie chose to devote his life to Raymond, teaching him everything about farm life, the two working side by side in a warm companionship.

Unable to leave totally the sport he loves, Fergie accepted a job as roving pitching instructor in the Reds' minor league. It kept him in touch with his baseball roots, while at the same time giving him more time at home with Raymond.

The lure of the diamond was great, though. In November, 1994, Jenkins once again donned his cap with the familiar Cubs' C on it. After putting out feelers with several other clubs, he was hired by the Chicago club as their pitching coach. Raymond was just a little older now, a little more independent, and it was time for both of them to get on with their lives.

Before Fergie was hired for this job, he told general manager Ed Lynch and Cubs' president Andy MacPhail about some ideas he had for training the pitchers. For one thing, he wanted to see less weight training. Pumping iron produced bulging biceps, but it also balled up the muscles. Fergie wanted to see the pitchers develop their muscles by throwing the ball a lot more and lifting weights a lot less. He also wanted to see them running, and playing more innings. It all sounded rather old-fashioned to the young players, but as Fergie said, it worked for Don Drysdale, Sandy Koufax, Tom Seaver, Ferguson Jenkins and many others who kept pitching winners for 20 years or more.

"There are two things in sport," Fergie once said. "Either you win or you lose. Life is like that, too. How you get through it depends on how strong your faith is." Few people are better qualified than Ferguson Jenkins to make a statement like that. As a major league pitcher, he knew all about winning and losing. In his personal life, too, he knew that he had made mistakes and had had to pay the consequences. Fate had also played a role in his development as a person, dealing him some painful blows that given him the choice of turning into bitterly angry person, or a mellow gentle one. That he chose the latter course is a credit to the man.

Even after that, Fate was not finished with Ferguson Jenkins. In May, 1999, while Fergie was in Dallas making a personal appearance at a golf classic, a tornado ripped through Lakeview Ranch. Fortunately, the eye of the tornado struck about a quarter mile from the ranch house, but a great deal of damage was done just the same. Lydia and her brother Derek were at the ranch at the time, and took shelter in a safe room in the basement. They came out of the event unscathed. The same could not be said for the rest of the ranch. Fences, trees, the patio, the deck and several loafing barns for the cattle were destroyed. It was another of life's setbacks to have to begin rebuilding the property which had just reached the stage of being comfortable and complete.

Fergie has had some good luck in recent years. For one thing, he found all of his good friends at the Fergie Jenkins Foundation. In 1998, he was playing in a golf classic at Wedgewood Golf and Country Club in Columbus, Ohio with a group of sports celebrities, including some golf pros. He'd been trying for some time to win a closest-to-the-pin contest, and on this occasion, he succeeded. The prize was a Harley Davidson motorcycle. Not much of a biking enthusiast, Fergie sold it for $10,000 and bought a new pickup truck for the farm.

23. The Worm in the Apple

Even when things go well, there are pitfalls. Fergie, like others before him, has made mistakes. However, he takes full responsibility for them, never blaming them on someone or something else. Just as important, he learns from his mistakes.

In 1973, he worked with George Vass, a sportswriter for the *Chicago Daily News* to produce a biography. The book was titled *Like Nobody Else*. Even those who didn't read the book were put off by the title. Fergie was publicly lambasted for giving the impression that he felt that he was above all the other excellent pitchers in the major leagues. Columnists, sportswriters and fans alike took him to task for this error in judgement. Fergie explained to the press that that wasn't it at all. He felt that he was in a class by himself because he wanted to be recognized for his own accomplishments, and not judged in comparison to the performance of others. Still, the title and the tone of the book made him sound boastful and arrogant. That was never the real Fergie. Even as a young and inexperienced baseball hero, he was a truly humble person. Of course he enjoyed the adulation of having his name in the sports headlines, being asked for autographs, and being treated royally. But he always knew that his success was based on a God-given talent and a great deal of hard work. He appreciated the accomplishments of other great pitchers such as Sandy Koufax, Tom Seaver, Juan Marichal and Bob Gibson, and never considered himself superior to them in any way. Still, once the damage had been done, it was difficult to dispel the impression which lingered.

When you ask Fergie about drugs, he freely admits that he used cocaine recreationally at one time. It was not a regular habit, just a fun-enhancing thing to do at parties. It was something everyone in that group of friends did at the time.

"You know things are wrong," Fergie admits, "but sometimes you do them anyway. Don't do wrong things!"

No one outside of his immediate circle of friends would have known or cared if it had not been for a series of events that happened in Toronto in August of 1980. It was just before the Texas Rangers were scheduled to play a three-game series with the Blue Jays. When the team arrived in Toronto, Fergie noticed that one of his bags was missing from the airport carousel. After a delay, he was told to go to the hotel with the other players, and the bag would be delivered when it was found. The bag was left in his room the next day, after Fergie had left with the team to go to the ballpark. He had no idea of its reappearance until he was escorted back to the hotel later.

After Fergie left for the ballpark, two customs officers searched his hotel room. Four grams of cocaine, two ounces of marijuana, a small amount of hashish and a hash pipe were found in the previously-missing bag. Just before the start of the first game of the series, officers arrived at Exhibition Stadium to arrest him - a humiliating experience in the presence of teammates and members of the press who were bound to turn it into a feeding frenzy.

"They even followed me into the shower room," Fergie recalls, "and watched me take a shower." Officers escorted him back to the hotel where they questioned him about the whereabouts of his hang-up bag. Unlike most of the other players, he never used a hang-up bag, and didn't know what they were talking about. At first, it was all very confusing. When confronted with the suitcase in which the drugs and paraphernalia were found, Fergie was mystified. The suitcase, which he had locked before leaving on the trip, contained his valuable pouch. He had not placed it there himself, and did not understand how anyone else could have put it there. Players' valuable pouches contained personal items such as their cash, credit cards, and passports. These pouches were normally kept in a locked safe room at the clubhouse. Only one person had the keys to that room, and all the players' valuable pouches were transported together when the team travelled. Fergie explained that he did not know how or when that pouch got into his locked suitcase. Until he was taken to his room by the customs officers, he had not seen the bag since it was put on the plane at the beginning of the trip.

Where had the bag been? Who could have unlocked it and put the drugs in it? Who tipped off the customs officers that there were drugs in the bag? Fergie had no answers. He was as much in the dark as the customs officers, and could offer no explanation. Nevertheless, he was charged with possession of illegal drugs and paraphernalia.

Mike Bennett from his hometown paper, the *Chatham Daily News*, recalls that he called Fergie at the hotel in Toronto as soon as he heard about the charge. He wouldn't have been surprised if Fergie had refused to take his call, but they talked and agreed to meet the next day at the ballpark where Fergie was scheduled to pitch. Fergie was eager to tell the people of Chatham what he knew, and assure them that he was not guilty. Bennett arrived at the park before game time and went to the dressing room as arranged. There was no Fergie in sight. Bennett asked "Where's Fergie?" No one replied. Then one of the players said "Yeah. Where is Fergie?" Rusty Staub and another first baseman rounded on Bennett and yelled "What the bleep do you think you're doing around here? We don't need this!"

"Hey, I'm from Fergie's home town, and he wants to talk to me," Bennett explained.

Gary Rasitch took Bennett aside and told him that the team had been told not to give any interviews, or even to mention Fergie's name.

"I had walked into a hornet's nest without realizing it," Bennett says. He learned that Fergie was still at the hotel, and was able to call him there. Fergie, almost tearful at times, told him to come to the hotel.

When Bennett got there, he could clearly see that Fergie was chastened and embarrassed. He told Bennett that he felt that he had let a lot of people down, including the team, his friends, his fans, and his country.

The person hurt most, however, was the one he wanted least to hurt, his father. Fergie Sr. had always regarded his son as a hero, and this was a blow to him. Of course he knew of his son's personal shortcomings, but he never dreamed that drugs would be an issue. It certainly had never been a problem during the teen years that parents worry about most.

"It was about two years before he believed me when I told him I didn't do it," Fergie recalls.

Even when speaking with his hometown media friend, Mike Bennett, Jenkins would only say that he couldn't tell the whole story. To this day, he will not lay the blame on anyone else or go into detail about what really happened. Those who know him believe he was the victim of a prank or a malicious act.

At the hearing in Brampton, Fergie had a lot of moral support. Kathy went into the hearing room with him, along with Gene Dziadura, friend Ron Hancock, his family doctor C.D. Keeley, and the mayor of Chatham, Doug Allin who had coached Fergie in Bantam League ball.

Fortunately for Fergie, the judge was sympathetic, although he clearly took the matter very seriously. He took into account the fact that the accused had a clean record up until that time, never even having had a traffic ticket; and that there was some question about how the illegal items got into the locked suitcase.

While waiting in the courtroom for the judge's decision, Fergie and his friends went "to hell and back", worrying about the outcome. When the judge returned from his chambers, he fixed his eyes on the defendant and gave him a stern lecture before telling him his decision. A total discharge was issued, with no fine or criminal charge on Fergie's record. This was a tremendous load off Jenkins' mind, for a criminal record could have prevented him from returning to the USA to work, and certainly would have ended his baseball career.

Although Jenkins neither confirms nor denies it, some believe that the cocaine and other drugs belonged to teammates who felt that, as a Canadian, he was less likely than they to be searched at the airport. If that is the case, it was an error of judgement on their part, and Jenkins became the victim. Or perhaps he was simply set up by someone who had a grudge against him. No one ever spoke up to take the pressure off Fergie. For his own part, Jenkins accepted the situation silently, yet with bitterness.

"I just couldn't watch my luggage all of the time," he says sadly. He recalls that "One of the hardest things was talking to my personal friends about it. I reminded them that when I came up to Canada to fish or hunt or visit with them, we never messed around with drugs. They knew that, and it was OK, but still a little humiliating."

In spite of the unconditional discharge, there were consequences. Fergie's outstanding record in the National League had made him a natural choice for induction into the Baseball Hall of Fame. A panel of sports writers and sports broadcasters choose candidates for this honour from outstanding players who have flawless records. Fergie's record on the diamond was impeccable, but this charge made a blot on his personal record that the experts couldn't ignore. For some years, they steered clear of Ferguson Jenkins. It wasn't until 1991 that they finally decided that, with no further misdemeanors on the record, he had paid his dues and deserved to be recognized.

More painful than this, however, was the fact that Bowie Kuhn, the baseball commissioner decided to hold his own hearing on the matter. Kuhn ordered Fergie to come to his office in New York City and make a sworn statement of the facts. Kuhn was an attorney, and although not practicing at that time, he should have known better. Fergie's lawyer Edward Greenspan pointed out that there would be a trial in Canada, and that at that point, his client had not been found guilty. Making a sworn statement at that time would have jeopardized the outcome of the trial. Kuhn insisted that the statement would be confidential, but Greenspan reminded him that even then Kuhn could not prevent the statement being subpoened and used in court against Jenkins.

Kuhn was not convinced. He told Fergie that unless he ignored Greenspan's advice and testified against himself, he would be suspended. Wisely, Jenkins listened to his lawyer. He felt that the way he was being treated was insulting to him personally, and to the Canadian legal system. Kuhn, unrepentant, suspended him from September 9th to 25th, and fined him $10,000. He also ordered him to take part in drug education program sponsored by the major league ball clubs. This involved making a videotape with two other major league ball players, talking about the dangers of using drugs.

As executive director of the Major League Baseball Players Association, Marvin Miller immediately asked for a hearing by an arbitrator. Ray Goetz, a law professor, was chosen to hear arguments by Kuhn and Greenspan a few days later. He was disgusted with Kuhn's arguments, and reinstated Fergie on the club's roster.

As far as Jenkins was concerned, the worst part was that for 20 days he was not able to suit up with the team, and during this period he lost some valuable pitching time.

Although he was angry and resentful of this treatment when the Canadian court had seen fit to give him an absolute discharge, Fergie paid the fine, took part in the drug education program, and made a public statement in which he asked his fans to forgive him. After that, he spent a lot of time speaking to young people's groups about the dangers of getting involved with drugs.

Painful as it was for both of them, Kathy stood beside her husband, physically and in spirit, throughout the ordeal.

The fans, on the whole, were very accepting. "Every so often, someone would throw a cigarette at me," Fergie remembers with a grin, "but that was about it." On one occasion, when he and some friends went from Canada to a NBA game in Detroit, he was detained briefly at the border, and wondered if this would be a pattern in the future. However, it never happened again.

There were other consequences, though. The incident did affect Fergie's career. The Texas Rangers weren't eager to have him back, and no one else was clamouring for him, either. The last place Chicago Cubs finally signed him for a year. Fergie rewarded them by winning 14 games that season. In return, the Cubs signed him again, this time for two years.

On another occasion, however, Jenkins was not so innocent, and he knew it. In 1970, when he was still very young and married to Kathy, Fergie became involved with a young woman who worked for an airline. The affair only lasted a couple of months, but the young woman gave birth to a daughter whom she named Felicia Ann Jenkins - Fergie's initials. Kathy's family got wind of this through the newspapers, and loyally protected her from the knowledge. However, it was inevitable that she would eventually hear about the affair and the baby. She was devastated, and a very bad time ensued for the Jenkins' marriage.

In his naivety, Fergie had gone to Chicago and paid for the hospital expenses of the mother and baby. "If I'd known more," he says, "I wouldn't have signed the papers at the hospital. But I did, and the story hit the headlines. I was a pretty popular player in Chicago at the time, so it made a big story."

The mother hired a lawyer to ask for support for the baby. By this time, Fergie was feeling thoroughly chastened, and was quite willing to co-operate. It was agreed that Fergie would put money into a trust fund for the child, and would not expect to be part of their lives. He has not seen the little girl since she was about a year old.

Says an old friend, "There have been times when I have felt like giving Fergie a good swift kick. This was one of them."

Mark Hebscher, George Chuvalo and Tim Twaddle at September Wine and Cheese party.

Jo Anne Molar, Johnny Bower and Fergie Jenkins march into the ballroom at a Wine and Cheese event.

24. The Third Dream

The creation of the Fergie Jenkins Foundation was the fulfillment of another dream that had been forming in the back of Fergie's mind for several years.

Ferguson Jenkins was the first celebrity to respond to Carl Kovacs' request and sign on for the Grimsby Sports Council's celebrity dinner. The others who signed on later were Gordie Howe, George Chuvalo, Ron MacLean, JoAnne Malar, Robert Esmie, Marilyn Bodogh and Bob Lenarduzzi.

The Celebrity Sports dinner was held on September 20th, 1997 at Place Polonaise in Grimsby. From noon to 5 p.m., the celebrities signed autographs and had their pictures taken with fans. It was an exciting day for youngsters involved in local sports, and it was equally exciting for their parents. Grimsby had never before seen such a gathering of famous athletes. In the evening, the huge dining room was packed for the dinner and presentation of awards. Throughout the evening, a silent auction of sports memorabilia was an added fund-raiser, with guests hurrying up and downstairs during breaks to see if they had been outbid on choice items.

Fergie greets Gordie Howe at the Sports Celebrity dinner, 1997

As a result of this event, $30,000 was raised for West Lincoln Memorial Hospital, Canadian Red Cross, Big Brothers/Big Sisters, the Grimsby Benevolent Fund, Niagara Victims Crisis Assistance and Referral Service, and West Niagara Palliative Care Service.

Fergie had arrived late for the autograph session on

Saturday afternoon because his plane was late getting in, so he stayed in Grimsby for an extra day. The next day, Carl Kovacs invited him to his home where they watched a baseball game on television, then Carl and his wife Nancy, took Fergie on a tour of the Niagara peninsula. They stopped off at some of the small wineries which make Niagara a prime tourist area, and took a look at the famous Falls. Fergie enjoyed this little adventure, and was delighted to see so many vineyards and little wineries throughout the peninsula. Later, as Carl Murray King and Fergie drove to Buffalo airport for Fergie's flight back to Oklahoma, Fergie asked if they could stop somewhere so that he could buy gifts for his

Hector Lopez and Bobby Bell at Wine and Cheese

family. They went into Walden Galleria in Buffalo to do some last minute shopping.

At the airport, the three had a snack and talked about events they could do in the future. There seemed to be good rapport at work here, and everyone had the same vision for future enterprises - the mission of helping other people. They agreed that there was so much that could be done through celebrity events like the sports dinner. As they said good-bye at the gate, Carl felt sure that Fergie was mulling it all over in his mind.

In the spring of the following year, Carl was invited to visit Fergie's ranch in Guthrie, Oklahoma with Fergie's long-time hunting companion, Murray King of Chatham. For a city lad like Carl, life on the Jenkins ranch was a revelation. Carl had the opportunity to feed calves with a bottle, and catch and club catfish in one of the two lakes on the ranch. While they were out fishing one day, they saw one of Fergie's cows fall off the dam into a lake. They immediately sped back to shore, jumped into a pickup truck, and were off to the rescue. Fergie quickly grabbed a rope, expertly twirled it around his head and roped the floundering cow. Then he tied the rope to the back of the truck and pulled the animal to safety. It was then that Carl realized that Fergie really is a country guy through and through. It's not just a persona put on for the public; it is the real Ferguson Jenkins.

During the visit at the ranch, Fergie talked often about doing a golf tournament or some other fund-raising events. He seemed to have a fixation on the topic, and was especially anxious to see

Fergie with an RCMP escort - Constables Yolanda McArthur and Willie Hubert - at Rockway Glen Golf Links, St. Catharines

these events organized within Canada. Finally Fergie said,

"You know, there's something I've had in the back of my mind for a long time. It's something I've always wanted to do, and you seem to be able to help me with it. Let's think about this. I'd like to establish a foundation so that all the money raised could go to charities, and those who donate can get receipts to help with their income tax. If we did that, the golf tournament and other any other events we decide to do could come under that umbrella."

Raising money to help others was not something new for Fergie. He'd taken part in many fund-rising events. Celebrities in all fields do it. Often, it's for the sake of the publicity it creates, but for many like Fergie, it is because of a true love of people, and an eagerness to use fame in a positive way. Frequently through the years, Fergie had made quick trips back to Chatham to take part in one charitable event or another. For example, on one occasion he flew from Atlanta to Detroit where he drove to London, Ontario. Car trouble made him three hours late arriving at his destination. Nevertheless, he attended a men's club meeting sponsored by the Canadian National Institute for the Blind, then visited the Crippled Children's Treatment Centre before attending a Sportsmen's dinner to raise funds for the Centre.

The idea of a foundation was not unique, either. Fergie's friend, Meadowlark Lemon, for example, has a foundation which includes a ministry to gang members, both professional and amateur athletes, Native Americans, and young people at risk throughout society. The words and example of athletes like Lemon and Jenkins can make a tremendous difference in the lives of others, especially young people who are searching for a beacon to guide them. A sports hero can be an angel in disguise.

The idea of the Fergie Jenkins Foundation caught fire. Everyone, including Lydia, believed that it should be pursued. As soon as Carl got home from Oklahoma, he called a meeting with Delight Davoli, a chartered accountant, and lawyer Jack Lovett. At first, Carl recalls, they were a little awed by the idea of working with a celebrity, but in the end they agreed to work on establishing the foundation. Delight set about getting charitable donation registration with the government, and handling the financial arrangements. Small organizations often wait for years to have their applications approved, but the application for the Fergie Jenkins Foundation Inc. went through quickly. No doubt it was due to Fergie's celebrity status, and the fact that he belongs to a visible minority. Nor was it harmed by the autographed glossy photos tucked in with the application as proof of his status in the sports world. Jack Lovett handled the legal work for incorporating the foundation.

Fergie wanted to be totally involved in the process. He read every document, checked every detail. It took many exchanges of documents between Fergie and Lovett's office and the Government of Canada before the agreement met everyone's satisfaction. Fax machines almost glowed as documents sped over the phone lines between Guthrie, Grimsby and the nation's capital. The foundation was formally registered on February 25th, 2000.

Two Cowboys - Eddie Shack and Fergie Jenkins

A website was immediately set up by John Oddi to let Fergie's fans everywhere know about the foundation's work and its activities. The website is kept up-to-date with events, new photos and news about the events and the charities involved. It can be seen at www.fergiejenkinsfoundation.org

One of the requirements for incorporation is that there must be a board of directors. Members of the board for the Fergie Jenkins Foundation were carefully chosen from businesses and organizations that the group had worked with, including the Canadian Baseball Hall of Fame.

At this point, Carl learned another lesson about Fergie. He is genuinely humble. Asked what title he'd like as head of the Foundation, Fergie felt that he should be "just one of the members, like everyone else".

"No way!" the others exclaimed. At their insistence, Fergie became Chairman of the Board.

The charities supported by the foundation in 2002 are the Canadian Red Cross, Canadian National Institute for the Blind (CNIB) Transitional Training Centre in Hamilton, Camp Maple Leaf, Y.M.C.A. Camp Wanakita, Child Refugees In Need of Effective Direct Aid (CRIED), West Niagara Second Stage Housing, the Canadian Diabetes Association, and the Ontario chapter of the Canadian Special Olympics.

The first charity golf tournament was held in September, 1999. Since then, each year in June, and again in September, the Fergie Jenkins Foundation has sponsored a fund-raising golf tournament at Rockway Glen Golf Course in St. Catharines. On the evening before the September tournament, the Foundation holds a Celebrity Wine and Cheese party attended by sports figures from all across Canada and the United States. At the beginning of the evening, the celebrities are piped into the ballroom, accompanied by two red-coated RCMP officers and are introduced to the crowd individually. Then the crowd of fans has the opportunity to chat with their sports heroes, and have memorabilia personally autographed for them. At the same time, a silent auction of sports-related items raises further funds for the Foundation's good causes.

Regulars at these events have been big names such as Gaylord Perry, Bob Gibson, Pierre Pilote, George Chuvalo, Johnny Bower, Bill "Space Man" Lee, Meadowlark Lemon, Eddie Shack, Angelo Mosca, Goose Gossage, Andy Bathgate, Joanne Malar and Harmon Killebrew.

Unfortunately, in September, 2001, some of the American celebrities who had confirmed attendance were unable to attend due to travel problems. Stan Mikita was delayed six-and-a-half hours in the airport in Chicago, and finally decided not to finish the trip. He sent ten autographed jerseys to the Foundation in apology. Bobby Bell and Johnny Orr could not attend because their flights were cancelled. Reggie Jackson was devastated at having lost two friends in the World Trade Centre attack, and felt he could not attend. A few celebrities cancelled out of sheer fear of flying, and no one faulted them for that.

However, about 17 American celebrities did attend in spite of the difficulties. Songwriter Rich Berg and TV producer Rick Hill drove from New York as an alternative to flying. So did infielder Armando Vazquez who in the 1940s played with the Cincinnati Clowns, the Indianapolis Clowns and the New York Cubans in the Negro Baseball Leagues.

Canadian celebrities were there in a solid show of solidarity for their American friends. The 2001 event began with Meadowlark Lemon, who is an ordained minister, offering a prayer for those lost in the terrorist attacks in the USA, and for peace throughout the world. There was also a minute's silence for two event "regulars" who had passed away during the previous month- Carl Brewer and Bill Stafford.

Board meetings for the Foundation are scheduled to coincide with events for the sake of convenience and economy. This also gives everyone the opportunity to gather for fun as well as business. There is always plenty of business to discuss, as the Foundation constantly has new projects under way.

For example, just in time for the 2001 Golf Classic in St. Catharines, artist Terry Quirk of London, England prepared a unusual collage of sketches of Fergie at different stages in his life and career. Quirk was drawn into the Foundation activities by his brother, Rick of Grimsby who has worked closely with Fergie's group from the start. There is a logical connection with London where Terry Quirk has his own graphic arts business but at the same time operates Sue's House, a cancer health counselling centre. Terry's first wife Sue died of cancer in 1984, and he has devoted his life to helping victims of this disease. When his brother asked him if he would help the Fergie Jenkins Foundation by drawing something, he quickly picked up his pen and set to work. The poster is based on photos of Fergie sent to the artist, and the work was done entirely in England. It's done in amazing detail, with an intuitive insight into Fergie Jenkins as a person, and a sense of humour that Fergie appreciates. Woven in among the life of Fergie Jenkins is recognition of all the sponsors who have helped the Foundation along the way.

It wasn't until the 2001 Golf Classic that Terry Quirk actually met the subject of his drawings in person.

"Actually, I'm more than pleased with the result," Terry says. "If I had one regret, it would be that I might have had a better photo of him as he is now. It isn't until you meet him that his gentility, his niceness, and his size really come through."

The posters are being sold as a fund-raiser for the Foundation which also supports the Canadian Cancer Society and the Canadian National Institute for the Blind in honour of Fergie's mother, Delores.

Also in the works for the Foundation is a baseball board game which will be available soon. In 1997, two Niagara wineries, Willow Heights and Thirty Bench, produced runs of wine in bottles with Fergie's picture on the labels. It was a great hit at the annual wine and cheese event.

Right from the start, an avid participant in the Foundation has been Rick Manners, a well-known wildlife artist who has his studio in the Old Stone Shop in Grimsby. Rick specializes in artwork on natural stone. As soon as he became involved with the Foundation's charitable works, he offered to immortalize Fergie on stone. His paintings of Fergie, often autographed, have drawn a great deal of attention at silent auctions held by the Foundation.

Being Introduced - from left to right: Ed Werenick, Marilyn Bodogh, Jim Sandlak, George Chuvalo and Mark Hebcher.

25. The Game is Easy - Life in Hard

Ferguson Jenkins' life has been full of highs and lows. There's been the high point of signing with a major league baseball team, and working up through the system to become a Hall of Fame celebrity. The adulation that goes along with being a sports star has turned many a young person to arrogance. Yet through all his awards and honours, Fergie has remained truly humble. He remains gracious to fans, even when they interrupt his meal in a hotel dining room. He never makes them feel that they are intruding, he never turns them away.

At the same time, he has known personal tragedies that have cause deep sadness and unhappiness. The loss of so many loved ones seems to be a burden no one should have to bear. Many people who are faced with such overwhelming challenges simply can't handle it. Sometimes they turn to self-destructive practices, or become cynical, arrogant or just plain hard to get along with.

Often, those who endure just one of the tragedies of Fergie's life are embittered forever, or crushed so that they can never again enjoy Life. Sometimes, they are so paralyzed by anger that they withdraw, never doing anything constructive again.

What has made Ferguson Jenkins different? He believes it all goes back to his parents who left him a legacy of faith and serenity.

"My father was a Catholic," he says, "but my mother was a Baptist. She took me to church regularly, and I attended Sunday School as well." Blessed with a good singing voice, on top of everything else, Fergie sang in two church choirs. One was at William Street Baptist Church which he attended with his mother, the other was nearby Park Street United Church where he attended Cub and Scout meetings.

No doubt the wholesome philosophy of the Scouting movement had an influence over the boy and the young man. Fergie is still very proud of the fact that he became a Queen's Scout, and he treasures his Queen's Scout ring, second only to his Hall of Fame rings.

Fergie's own philosophies of life and baseball are simple. Work hard. Do your best. Help others. Keep the faith. Realize that there are "no guaratees". He has learned many lessons in Life, and he takes them all to heart. For example, he knows that it is important to respect life because it is very precious, and can so easily be taken away. You have to do the best you can and as much as you can while you're alive. That's why you're on this planet. While you're responsible for yourself, once you have a spouse and a family you're also partly responsible for them.

At the same time, Fergie is painfully aware that you can't always prevent bad things from happening to the people you love. You can't be with them every minute, so you have to trust them to a Higher Power.

Going to church with his mother made a life-long impression on Fergie. He still attends church when he can. At home in Guthrie, it's the First Baptist Church, although he often stops in at St. Mary's Catholic Church just to sit quietly and think. But there is more to Fergie's faith than simple church-going.

He was always interested in the Fellowship for Christian Athletes (FCA) to which he was introduced when he began playing major league baseball. Between batting practice and a game, there would often be a brief FCA meeting with a short inspirational testimonial. Fergie found this helpful, both in his career on the mound and in his personal life. He is still involved with FCA which was founded in 1934 by Branch Rickey, Don McClanen and Paul Benedum to create a wholesome atmosphere in sports at all levels.

After Cindy and Samantha died, he decided that dwelling on all the bad things that had happened to him would only be detrimental to the rest of his own life. He remembered his mother, in her last days, telling him to live his own life. He made up his mind that he would follow that advice now. He devoted himself entirely to raising his adopted son, Raymond. And to helping others in a very proactive way.

Was he disappointed at never having the opportunity to play in a World Series? Of course he was. It's every Big League baseball player's ultimate dream. It would have been the icing on the cake.

But Ferguson Jenkins does not dwell on disappointment.

"My career had a lot of great things happen. Cooperstown was my World Series."

One of the things that has never bothered Fergie is the aspect of fame that often bothers other celebrities. That is the demands that fans sometimes make on their favourite stars. Jenkins has never been upset by people who stop him to ask for an autograph. "I regard it as a compliment," he says. "The public is part of my life. Fans are important to me, especially the kids. Every time a kid comes up to me with a bubblegum card and asks me to sign it, I think of the money he has spent for the card, and how he waited for the opportunity to ask me to autograph it. I know what it is like. I used to collect cards myself"

Retirement for Ferguson Jenkins has not involved sitting around and taking it easy. Work on the ranch is hard, and it has to be done every day. In addition to the horses and cattle, there are 90 acres of winter wheat, alfalfa, and rye grass. There is a foreman at Lakeview Ranch, but whenever he is home, Fergie works at whatever needs to be done at the time. The cattle are Angus, these days, although at various times, Fergie has raised Charolais and Limousin as well. Lakeview Ranch's specialty, though, is Appaloosas. Fergie bought his first Appaloosa from a friend in Katant, Pennsylvania. The horse's name was Sassy Socks. In time, Fergie's herd grew to 30 horses. Now, there are just 11 at Lakeview Ranch.

There's still plenty of travel in retirement. Fergie could be in St. Catharines, Ontario for a foundation board meeting one day, back in Oklahoma for a couple of days, then off to New York City to make an appearance at a sports card show. He could be at a Canadian Baseball Hall of Fame golf game and induction, or a celebrity wine and cheese event in the Niagara peninsula.

These days, it is quiet on the farm. Just Fergie and Lydia live there now. Raymond lives in Streamwood, Illinois and attends college in Chicago. He is studying computer art, and does freelance pastel and pencil drawing. Fergie's daughters still live in Chatham, and they all keep in touch frequently. Kimberly, the youngest, works in Chatham. Kelly and Delores are married. In the fall of 2000, Delores transformed Fergie into a grandfather when her son, Kaleb Matthew was born. That's a brand new phase in Ferguson Jenkins' life.

Fergie and Lydia first met in 1969 when she was a showgirl at the Tropicana Hotel in Las Vegas. At the time, Fergie was living in Scottsdale during spring training. When he and some friends went to a club one night, he spotted the beautiful 6' brunette with a "covey of quail" - that is, a group of girl friends. He introduced himself and bought her a drink. Later, he and his friend Ted Savage were invited to her home.

Fergie laughs when he recalls that occasion. "Here were two black men getting out of a rented car in her driveway. The neighbours must have been staring. There weren't many black people around in that Scottsdale suburb!" He became friends with the family, however, and took Lydia's younger brother, Derek, to a ballgame. Then they lost touch.

In 1992, Fergie was in Sun City, Arizona doing an appearance for new model homes. There was an advertisement for the event on television. When Lydia saw it, she decided to go with a friend to see if the Ferguson Jenkins on the screen was the same guy she remembered from 22 years before.

When Fergie saw her across the room, he recognized her immediately, but couldn't remember her name or where they had met. He went over and said "Excuse me, but I know you from somewhere." Lydia and her friend started to giggle.

"What's so funny?" he asked, as he began to recall their previous meeting. "Don't you remember going on a date with me?"

"Sure I do," Lydia replied. "You took my brother Derek to a ballgame and gave him a ball."

"Look, I have to stay here for a while yet," Fergie said. "But don't leave. Please don't leave." And she didn't.

Lydia and Fergie were married on Lakeview Ranch in December, 1993, with family and closest friends in attendance.

Growing up in the air-conditioned atmosphere of Arizona and

Nevada, Lydia is not an outdoors person. She likes to ride, but

Wedding day for Fergie and Lydia at Lakeview Ranch in Guthrie, 1993

doesn't care for gardening or outdoor work. Instead, she spends most of the time indoors, away from the Oklahoma humidity that bothers her allergies. In her home office, she looks after the taxes, pays the bills, and performs all the duties of a private secretary.

One Sunday afternoon when Fergie wanted to watch football, Lydia turned off the television set and said "We have to sit down and figure out what to do." As she saw it, there was no sense in Fergie paying for a manager to arrange his appearances when she was right there at the ranch all the time and was already doing most of the office work. She knew she could easily handle the job. For five per cent of the gross, she told Fergie, she'd take on the job.

Fergie said, "Okay. Give it a try."

Lydia formed Lydia Farrington Enterprises. They worked out a fee schedule and other details of the business. Then Lydia prepared an information spiel that she would give when interested parties telephoned - rates for various types of appearances etc. She practiced over and over again until she felt sure she knew it perfectly. Then came the moment when she answered her first call to Lydia Farrington Enterprises. Fergie was in the background listening, and trying hard not to laugh out loud. Lydia flubbed her lines four times before getting the message straight. "I was so nervous!" she recalls. Actually talking to the public was not the same as rehearsing in an empty room, she discovered. But practice makes for perfection. Dealing with clients soon became as natural as breathing for Lydia. Nevertheless, it is a huge undertaking, because Ferguson Jenkins is still very much in demand, and has a busy schedule of appearances all over the continent. When he travels on behalf of the Foundation, Continental Airlines supports Fergie by giving him special rates. Often, however, he is "on the road" travelling to sports memorabilia shows, exhibition games or other events. His days at home on Lakeview Ranch are precious and very much appreciated.

Lydia Farrington Enterprises eventually wrapped up, and Bob Allen in Milwaukee now handles Jenkins' personal appearance bookings. Lydia is Fergie's personal secretary, and refers queries about appearances to Allen. Often, she enjoys travelling with Fergie to special events.

26. What Makes A Winner?

One reason for Ferguson Jenkins' lasting success was the fact that he took care of himself. He knew that as long as he looked after his arm and the rest of his body, he would be able to continuing performing at the highest level. It's a lesson that many a celebrity has failed to learn, and it's often been the downfall of a great career.

Fergie credits his parents' upbringing with the confidence and inner calm that have been as asset to him throughout life. He always believes that if he does his best, everything will work out. So in tight situations on the ball diamond, he always knew he had done everything possible in training, he was going to perform well now, and the results would justify all the effort. The same philosophy has carried through in his personal life.

Having been brought up in a wholesome atmosphere made it much easier for Fergie to resist the temptation to "goof off". He knew that even during the off-season, he had to continue to train for optimum fitness. As he sometimes said, he knew that he just couldn't afford to "burn the candle at both ends." His career was important to him, and he worked hard to maintain it.

Ferguson Jenkins has always believed in learning from his own mistakes, and he admits he has made plenty of them. In 1983, he said "Every time you learn something, it helps you - maybe a week, a month, maybe a year from now. Once you stop learning - let me tell you - you're going to be in the second row looking at somebody else playing."

Gene Dziadura, Fergie's mentor, trainer and friend before and throughout his professional career always had the highest praise for his greatest baseball "find". He knew that determination, focus and hard work had paid off for Fergie. Perhaps the most important word there is focus. Fergie found that he could walk out onto the field with thousands of fans yelling, and he could block it all out to concentrate on the job at hand. He discovered that some players used earplugs or wads of cotton to shut out the distracting sounds from the stands, but for him, that wasn't necessary.

Although Fergie is a personable fellow, there have been times when fans and the press thought he was cold and distant. Going into a game, he would seldom smile or exchange jokes with teammates or fans. One journalist who first met him in the locker room took an instant dislike to him, only to find him an entirely different, unmistakably likeable person after the game. For Fergie made a point of focusing his attention completely on the job at hand until it was finished. He needed that concentration, for often before a game he was nervous and anxious.

"Outside I can look cold turkey, but inside everything's jumping around," he once admitted. "I often have butterflies in my stomach when I go out there to pitch."

During the ball season, Fergie never ate a big breakfast. A glass of milk and a vitamin pill were about his limit. After a game, he wanted a big meal, including plenty of meat. In the off-season, he enjoyed a hearty breakfast of hot cereal, then bacon and eggs or waffles with sausage. In his retirement, he's gained a few pounds, but he still likes to "eat healthy".

"He lasted," Dziadura said, "because he took care of himself. After the season, he rested until November, then he began to train in earnest in January for the season ahead."

Fergie is equally lavish in his praise of Dziadura who is still his close friend. "Without his support and encouragement," Jenkins says, "I doubt that I would have ever become a professional ball player."

During his career, Jenkins never got the recognition he deserved. Although he was a big star in baseball, he had very few endorsements. One was the sum of $500 for throwing a baseball into a car-seat cover. A restaurant in the midwestern USA offered a specialty called a Fergie Burger. But no large corporations - not even Canadian ones - approached him for product endorsements. This is rather surprising, for other Canadian sports figures such as Bobby Orr, Wayne Gretsky, skier Nancy Greene, Elvis Stojko and Maurice "Rocket" Richard have appeared in advertising. With his fine appearance and articulate manner of speaking, Fergie would have been the ideal celebrity to appear on a cereal box or in a car commercial. Was it because he never had an agent who promoted him aggressively enough? Or was he because he was a black Canadian? Perhaps the answer lies simply in the fact that during his era in the spotlight, there were so many other outstanding pitchers who won recognition by pitching in the World Series that Ferguson Jenkins was overlooked. The fact remains that in spite of his amazing professional record, Fergie never had the opportunities that have come to other sports stars. When asked about this aspect of his career, Jenkins humbly admits that it would have been nice to have had some endorsements.

One of Fergie's favourite expressions regarding his life or anyone else's is "No guarantees." In other words, there are no guarantees of success or happiness. It takes hard work, both physically and mentally, to get through life's turbulence.

When Larry Jansen moved from San Francisco to Chicago to work with the Cubs pitchers, he quickly identified Ferguson Jenkins as the type of pitcher he called a Master. In Jansen's mind, that put Fergie in the same category as Lefty Grove, Carl Hubbell, Bob Feller, Warren Spahn, Sandy Koufax and Don Drysdale. What made them Masters? Jansen's reply was "They were blessed with two very big 'C"s, control and a deep desire to always be competetive." That description fit Jenkins to a "T".

"Fergie has just one thought in mind when he's throwing off the mound or in the bullpen, and that's a desire to concentrate on throwing strikes." There is no doubt that control figured prominently in Jenkins' success as a pitcher. But it was not control that came easily. It was the result of serious study of the dynamics of the baseball, endless practice to keep his skills honed to perfection, and determination to focus totally on pitching..

Pitchers, like other practitioners of a skill, each have a unique philosophy. Sandy Koufax, for example, once said "Pitching is...the art of instilling fear." Fergie's philosophy was a gentler one.

Early baseballs were made out of scraps of leather, sewn together with a filling of rags or whatever was handy. They were usually created by the local shoemaker. As the game progressed, so did the need for a better ball. After all, a pitcher of Ferguson Jenkins' calibre needs a ball that will do justice to his skills, travelling straight and true. Jenkins recalls that the National League balls had black stitching and lettering, while American League balls were identified by blue printing and stitching. American League balls also had slightly heavier seams so that the pitcher could get a better grip on the ball. Minor league balls featured a combination of red and blue stitching.

Nowadays, the circumference and weight of baseballs are carefully regulated. The outer covering is made from two pieces of white horsehide or cowhide, sewn together with red or blue stitching. The inside core is cork wrapped in two layers of rubber and yarn. The balls are tested by being shot against a wall. In to-day's Big Leagues, it is important to have uniformity and quality. Those balls have to be able to take a lot of punishment.

Like a good baseball, a good bat is also essential for the professional. In the major leagues, aluminum bats are never used. All the bats are made from kiln-dried mountain ash which has been carefully crafted for the professional. The history of the professionally designed bat goes back to 1884 when Bud Hillerich was watching a game played by the Louisville Eclipse team. The team's star, Pete Browning, was in a deep slump; the last straw came when he broke his favourite bat. After the game, Hillerich told Browning that he would make a new bat for him at his father's woodworking shop where he was employed. They worked together to create the perfect bat for Browning. The next day, Browning went three-for-three with the new bat. It pulled him out of his slump, and gave the Hillerich woodworking shop a brand new direction. The elder Mr. Hillerich protested at first, but when the Louisville Slugger became the bat of choice on the baseball field, he had to give in.

Most pitchers don't have their own bats because they are not notorious for being great hitters. However, when Jenkins had hit a few homeruns, the Hillerich & Bradsby Company came to him and said "We're going to make a Louisville bat for you." So Fergie became the registered owner of the D143 flame-treated bat. It's

42" long, and weighs 32 ounces. Each season, the company made about two dozen of the bats for Jenkins. He would use about half a dozen of them, and keep the rest to autograph for gifts and door prizes for special events. Jenkins' bats are still being made for promotional uses. They appear every year at the Fergie Jenkins Foundation silent auctions.

Fergie didn't have to resort to the handmade adaptations that ball players often use to make a bat suit them exactly. Some shave the bat down a little to make it fit the hands perfectly. This is quite legal, although inserting cork into the core of the bat is not; the umpire can ask to inspect the bat if he suspects cork or any other illegality.

Batters are taught to hold the bat with the trademark facing up. There is a reason for this. Bats are made with the trademark branded on the side of the bat nearest the flat of the grain so that the strongest part of the bat will hit the ball. Yogi Berra wouldn't conform to this, always batting with the trademark facing the pitcher, so Hellerich and Bradsby began intentionally stamping his bats on the wrong side.

When Casey Stengel told Hank Aaron to hold the bat so that he could read the label, Aaron is quoted as saying "Didn't come up here to read. Came up here to hit."

When Fergie Jenkins' career as a pitcher wrapped up, he was only the fourth pitcher in baseball history to win more than 100 games in both leagues. The three who came before him were Cy Young, Jim Bunning and Gaylord Perry. Since then, only two more have joined this elite group of pitchers. They are Nolan Ryan and Dennis Martinez.

Yet, in spite of his many achievements and honours, Fergie never received the recognition he deserved. One reason for this is that he never pitched for a World Series team. It certainly wasn't from lack of ability or effort. While the pitcher is a very important part of the team, he can't do the job without the help of everyone else on the team. While Fergie feels that he was blessed with wonderful team-mates, many of whom became lifelong friends, there's still a sense of loss that all of them together were never able to make it to the World Series.

Pitching coach Fergie Jenkins with the 1987 Pan Am Games team that went on to the Olympics

In a sense, though, Fergie has made it to the World Series, the World Series of Life. He continues to encourage young players to hone their skills and strive for excellence. In speaking to an aspiring young pitcher, he recently said "Keep working at it, and don't get discouraged. I was 21 before I mastered the slider, and when I did, well, it was pretty nasty. Your will have to work hard, but it will be worth it". In fact, Fergie's slider was notable. In his book *Kings of the Hill: An Irreverent Look at the Men on the Mound"* Nolan Ryan lists Ferguson Jenkins as #2 on his list of Top Ten Pitchers With the Nastiest Slider, topped only by J.R. Richard.

27. What Does a Retired Hall of Fame Pitcher do?

He keeps right on pitching, of course. Not in the major leagues, but with the major leagues. It is every professional's ambition to pass along his special skill and knowledge to the youngsters coming up through the ranks. Ferguson Jenkins wanted to do exactly that. For many years, he had the responsibility of the farm near Chatham, and his young family. He kept in touch with the baseball scene in southwestern Ontario by being a player/coach with the London Majors who played in the Inter-County Major Baseball League. He pitched for the Majors for two seasons after retirement. In 1987, he was asked to be pitching coach for Canada's Pam Am Games Team. This was a successful venture, because the team went on to compete in the Olympics. But Fergie always wanted to do more.

In 1988, Fergie was pitching coach for the Texas Rangers' Triple A Oklahoma City 89ers. His philosophy of optimism and faith in his fellow Man permeated his treatment of the men he worked with. Tony Fossas, a player who had been in the minor leagues for ten years, felt discouraged and was ready to give up when he was called up to the Rangers' camp that year. After watching Fossas for a while, Fergie told the player that he liked what he saw, and if Fossas could focus on getting left-handed hitters out, he could have a good career in the major leagues.

"No one had ever said anything like that to me before," Fossas said. "In ten long years, no one ...had ever expressed confidence in me. It turned me around. I went to the minors, but that June I was in Texas, in the big leagues after all. Amazing, really, just a few positive words in my ear and...I had a purpose, a goal...I had confidence."

Being able to help younger players as pitching coach of the Texas Rangers' Triple-A team, and later for the Cincinnati Reds was the fulfilment of another of Fergie's dreams. Stepping back into the world of baseball after retirement opened new opportunities to use his years of skill and knowledge.

Spring of 1995 saw Fergie back with the Chicago Cubs, this

time as pitching coach. He had some slightly different ideas from those usually adopted by pitching coaches of that time.

"I've got a program I'd like to implement," he said "back to the 60s." He felt that young pitchers were lifting too many weights, balling up their biceps.

"We're not football players, we're baseball players. An arm stays strong and muscle tone develops by throwing that 5.30 ounce baseball - a lot." Fergie was thinking back to the days when he was working out regularly with Gene Dziadura, developing strength, speed and accuracy by constantly throwing the ball. To his critics, he pointed out that the great pitchers of the 60s - Don Drysdale, Sandy Koufax, Tom Seaver, Gaylord Perry - were highly successful for up to 20 years, and none of them ever lifted weights.

Fergie also wanted a four-man rotation, instead of a five-man rotation, so that each pitcher would get in plenty of hard work during the 90-game season. The Cubs' management liked most of his ideas, although the four-man rotation seemed a little extreme. Still, Fergie tried to be flexible in his dealing with both players and management. Bullying was simply not part of this soft-spoken man's style.

The honeymoon lasted about 18 months. Then in September, 1996 the club announced that Fergie was fired. There were different ideas about why this happened. Perhaps his philosophy as a pitching coach just wasn't the same as that of the ball club management, although the Cubs' pitching roster was sixth in the National League that year. Some writers speculated that there was a disagreement between the club manager and one of the pitchers, and Fergie sided with the pitcher. No one knows for sure. Disappointed? Of course he was.

"I'm not bitter," he told the press. "I've been hired to be fired before. It's nothing new." Fergie accepted the matter with typical equanamity.

His reputation as a great pitching coach had earned him the title of National League honorary coach for the July 11th, 1995 All-Star game hosted by the Texas Rangers at The Ballpark in

Arlington. Retired Ranger Nolan Ryan was the honorary coach for the American League team.

Jenkins is active in the Major League Baseball Players Alumni Association, travelling extensively to make speeches and appearances that raise money for the association's charitable works. The MLBPA was founded in 1982 to promote the game of baseball, to involve former major league players in community activities, and to inspire to-day's youth through positive sports images. Of the 6,000 men who have played professional baseball in the major leagues, about 2800 are registered members of the association.

When he moved to his adopted home, Oklahoma, Fergie became totally involved in the life of the community. In 1994, he helped organize the Oklahoma Sports Museum in Guthrie. As good things often do, it came about in an unusual way. A number of local businesses displayed memorabilia from Oklahoma sports celebrities. For example, a restaurant had the autographed batting glove owned by major league catcher Johnny Bench. Nearby, model bats of eight Oklahoma Baseball Hall of Famers were embedded in the wall of a bank.

In October, 1992, Richard Hendricks, the supervisor of one of the schools in Guthrie, invited ex-Globetrotter Hubert "Geese" Ausbie to come and speak to the students about drugs and sports. Geese, knowing that Fergie lived in Guthrie, invited him to come along and take part in the program. Ausbie had a lot of memorabilia from his time with the Harlem Globetrotters, and he commented that he wished there was a good place to display it. Hendricks, Ausbie and Jenkins talked about how young people in the community could be made more aware of the outstanding contributions of Oklahoma athletes. Also, they felt that it was very important to tell the youngsters how to succeed in sports without getting involved with drugs or alcohol. In the end, a committee was formed. At a public meeting in January, 1993, more than 20 of the people in attendance put down $25 each toward a new museum. It was an encouraging start.

The city of Guthrie was doing extensive redevelopment of a

district called the Tannery. Hendricks saw the possibilities there, and the committee was able to purchase three buildings which became the Oklahoma Sports Museum and Hall of Fame.

Within a short time, the buildings housed about 5,000 items donated by athletes who were born in Oklahoma, or who have lived in the state for a major part of their sports careers. This includes dozens of famous sports figures such as Warren Spahn, Mickey Mantle, Troy Aitkins and Shannon Miller.

When the committee decided to give an award for the best left-handed pitcher, the honour was named the Warren Spahn Award. In 1999 and again in 2000, Randy Johnson was the winner of the large bronze trophy created especially for the museum by artist Shawn Gray.

This non-profit venture in Guthrie has made the community more aware of its outstanding Oklahoma athletes, and of the fact that many of them have succeeded by living positive, drug-free lives. Through the museum, Jenkins inspires young people with his talks about his career, and about the pitfalls of using drugs and alcohol. He is also the Oklahoma Alzheimer Association's celebrity host at fund-raising events within that state.

But Jenkins' dreams are not all for himself. Sometimes, he works at fulfilling other people's dreams. For example, Fergie often has been to Arizona to take part in programs at fantasy baseball camps, where guests pay handsomely to fulfill their dreams of being involved with Big League baseball. The Fantasy Camps were started by Randy Hundley in 1982 in Scottsdale, Arizona where campers were invited to play against the 1969 Chicago Cubs team. Nineteen of the 25 members of the 1969 team turned out to give the campers the thrill of a lifetime. Jenkins enjoyed the event so much that he has been back every year.

"They're fun for everyone, the campers and the players," says Fergie. "Not only that, but a lot of business deals are made, because you have people from all sorts of businesses coming together and getting acquainted."

Fans who usually are middle-aged men can actually play with and against some of the baseball "greats" like Hall of Famer

Ferguson Jenkins. Participants also have the opportunity to set up teams, plans schedules, and get an inside look at what goes on in administering a ball club. Every day, they have double-header seven-inning ball games. Campers get five outs, the pros they play with only get two. Most of the campers have never put on a uniform, never swung a bat, never slid into a base, although they've watched their heroes do it hundreds of times. For them, it is a great thrill to go out on the field and play with the men they've admired from the grandstand or an easy chair in front of their television set.

Among the charitable events Fergie has enjoyed was the National Oldtimers Baseball Classic, an annual five-inning game to benefit retired baseball players. In the 1990 Classic, Fergie pitched a scoreless inning for the National League at Pilot Field. The National League defeated the American League 3-0 in this game. It was just one of the many seniors' or oldtimers' games that Fergie has enjoyed.

In August, 2000, Fergie Jenkins along with some of the foundation board members were travelling by helicopter to visit board member John Outlaw and his wife. On the way, it was arranged for them to stop off at Camp Maple Leaf, a camp operated by Hamilton East Community Services for disadvanaged city children. Located on a 104-acre island in Pigeon Lake in the Kawarthas, the camp was founded in 1955 by a group from the Canadian Council of War Veterans Association who wanted a living memorial to their fallen comrades. They felt that a camp for underprivileged children of all races and creeds would promote greater understanding of people, thus giving meaning to the cause for which their comrades made the supreme sacrifice. The camp was taken over by Hamilton East Community Services in 1996. The plan for the August, 2000 visit was for a brief stop to talk to Fergie about the establishment of a baseball field at the camp. A ball field was the one facility lacking on the island, and as a sponsoring celebrity, Fergie was very interested in the project. It had been arranged that Jenkins Field would be established on the island for the campers, and on this visit, Fergie would turn the first sod. But far more than that happened. Fergie spoke to the children about achievement in whatever field of endeavour they choose, and he took time to answer their questions. This fit in perfectly with the camp's mandate to instill respect for others, self-discipline and self-respect in children who might otherwise not have the guidance they need to become successful adults.

Afterwards, Jenkins signed a baseball for each child. Volunteers were standing by to hand out the balls, but Fergie turned that idea down flat.

Fergie chats with campers at Camp Maple Leaf, Pigeon Lake, Ontario - Hamilton East Community Services

"No," he said, "I want to do that myself." This personal touch won him the admiration of both children and adults in attendance.

A week later, he participated in the Commitment For Kids promotion at Centre Mall in Hamilton. He acted as celebrity sports coach for Oldies 1150's personality Jason Farr, doing interviews, autographing T-shirts and refereeing a pickup basketball game that featured former regional chairman Terry Cooke. During the event, Jenkins presented Camp Maple Leaf with a cheque for $7,000 raised at a recent golf tournament.

Hamilton East Community Services' fund-raising co-ordinator Doug Kay is lavish in his praise of Jenkins. "We asked another sports celebrity to take part in one of our events, and he wanted $15,000," Doug recalls. "Fergie spent all that time at the camp, and at the mall and asked for nothing. All the money raised went directly to our fund-raising." That's what the Fergie Jenkins Foundation is all about.

August 2001 was a replay of the Camp Maple Leaf event when Fergie visited Camp Wanakita in the Haliburton Highlands. He was impressed to see so many children, including disabled youngsters, enjoying sports. Once again, it was a thrill for him to autograph and distribute baseballs, especially for ten young baseball fans who were at the camp from Japan.

In the spring of 2001, Ferguson Jenkins was chosen as one of the first subjects for a new TNN series called *Profiles*. Tracy Britnell of Bradford Productions says he was chosen because his whole life has been a story in itself. "He is the best baseball player this country has produced. His life

Eager campers at the ground breaking for Fergie Jenkins Field - Hamilton East Community Services

from childhood on has been an interesting saga which continues to this day," said Britnell.

This interesting saga does continue. In September, 2001, Fergie was invited to Chatham for another honour. The original gymnasium at John McGregor Secondary School was renamed the Ferguson Jenkins Auditorium in a special ceremony. This was the gym where Fergie played a lot of basketball and volleyball during his two years at this high school. In those days, John McGregor offered only Grades Nine and Ten to students.

In his speech to the entire school, Fergie told a multitude of stories about his life as a major league ballplayer. He also pointed out that his dreams have come true, and that the students can also make their dreams a reality.

"With some hard work and perseverance, I think you can reach your goals, but you gotta have dreams...if you can't dream, you can't imagine that you can do things." He urged students not to be deterred from their goals, but to concentrate on being the best person possible.

The auditorium was so quiet you could hear a pin drop; the students were enthralled by Fergie's message.

Fergie with daughters Kimberly and Delores, and grandson Kaleb

Kimberly

Kelly

28. What The Future Holds

Nothing is ever certain in this life, but on September 26th, 2001 it looked as though a new phase in Jenkins' career had begun. On that day, at a press conference in Vancouver, his appointment as Commissioner for the new Canadian Baseball League was announced. This new position in the baseball world presented a new challenge for Fergie. The popularity of baseball as a community and a professional sport has been waning in North America. It would be an interesting new venture for him to instill in Canadian players the enthusiasm that provided him with the opportunity to excel in a professional sport.

In its inaugural season beginning with spring training in April, 2002, it was planned that the league would begin with eight teams, each with a 22-man roster and a 72-game schedule. There would be a draft, and the players would be chosen mostly from Canada, although there would be some from Latin America, the Far East and Australia as well. Although the first teams would be in cities such as Red Deer, Saskatoon, Regina, Abbostford, Kamloops, Lethbridge and Nanaimo, in time it was planned that there would be teams all across Canada, in Pacific, Central and East divisions. A total of about 25 cities have been identified as possible locations for CBL franchises.

"There's a good talent pool out there," Fergie explains. "A lot of Canadians are playing ball, and this will give them the opportunity to excel. The league is actually the spin-off of the independent Canadian leagues that have always existed. In this league, the imports will be Americans, rather than the other way around."

Although there are now many Canadians playing baseball at the college level, there are only 13 Canadians in the major leagues at present. In recent years, major league teams in the U.S.A. simply haven't invested the time or money to send scouts into Canada. At one time, they did more scouting in this country, but found that they lost a lot of good athletes to hockey, among them Michel Dion, Denis Potvin and Jean Potvin. This means that the

U.S. Leagues been missing out on a lot of good talent, and Canadians players haven't had the opportunity to advance in the professional field.

"In my heart," says Fergie, "I believe there are a lot of Canadian youngsters that don't get the opportunity because major-league scouts pass them over." Once the Canadian Baseball League becomes operational, that may change.

Steve Avila, the new league's vice-president and director of baseball operations, pointed out that there are 600 players at colleges in Canada, and 400 Canadians playing at college level in the United States. There should be no problem at all in filling up team rosters.

In recent years, as AA and AAA baseball teams moved across the border by American owners, some excellent ballparks in Canada have been sitting idle in the summer. The new league would enable those parks to open again. The teams' home cities will be no more than 300 or 400 miles apart so that players can travel by bus. This will be cheaper and more convenient that air travel. Games will be played on weekends, but the players won't be idle the rest of the week. They'll be busy getting the intensive, professional training and instruction that minor league players don't get once they've started playing.

Spring training was scheduled to begin in April, 2002 with Fergie Jenkins in command as commissioner. However, less than two months before training was to begin, two teams withdrew from the league, and there were difficulties with facilities and scheduling. Rather than go ahead with only six teams for the 2002 season, league management decided to postpone spring training until 2003. When the new league does get under way, the prize at the end of the season will be the Jenkins Cup.

CBL director of communications Alex Klenman admitted "Maybe we were a little overexpectant, naïve perhaps that we could get it done. At this time, it's pretty clear that we can't get it done for 2002." When the league does get under way in 2003, it is expected that it will include cities in eastern Canada as well as those in British Columbia, Alberta and Saskatchewan.

Meanwhile, the League has plans to send out a pair of barnstorming exhibition teams that will play 20 to 60 games.

Tony Riviera, founder of CBL who is also president and CEO, said that "As much as our enthusiasm and effort has carried us, it has become clear that there isn't enough time to roll this out the way we envisioned for 2002. We have returned all the money we've received for season seats for 2002, and are proceeding with our revised plans...We are committed to giving Canadian fans the brand of baseball they deserve, and nothing less." Riviera added that Fergie Jenkins was chosen for the job of commissioner because they were looking for someone who understands baseball and has ties to Canada. He feels sure that Fergie will bring to his new job the passion for baseball and the passion of being a Canadian.

"Fergie will be working with us to help position and maintain the league's commitment as Canada's premier professional baseball venue," says Riviera. "He'll be working on the rules and regulations, and helping us to make professional baseball in Canada truly fun."

On November 20th, 2002 at The New Theatre in Toronto, the Canadian Baseball League announced its plans to launch the season in May with eight teams, four in the east, four in the west. They are the Niagara Stars, London Monarchs, Montreal Royales, Trois-Rivieres Saints, Saskatoon Legends, Calgary Outlaws, Kelowna Rockets, and Victoria Capitals. The league will play a 16-week season of 72 regular games, plus a special Canada Day game. The Jenkins Cup will be awarded in September. So Canada's own professional baseball league is finally on its way.

Fergie looks forward to this new phase in his life. He knows that the job will once again involve plenty of travel during the season, but he's used to that. He's been travelling the continent in all directions since he was 19 years old. This time, the burden may be lightened somewhat by a new place of residence for Lydia and Fergie Jenkins. The dust and humidity of Oklahoma have always bothered Lydia's allergies. In addition, with all of Fergie's new "hats", the care of so much land and so many livestock has become overwhelming. In the near future, Lydia and Fergie plan to relocate in the cooler, dryer climate of Colorado. This will put them nearer the centre of the continent, and closer to almost everywhere Fergie will need to go. Always a country lad at heart, Fergie still wants to own a ranch where he can have a few horses and dogs, but this will definitely be a smaller spread than Lakeview Ranch.

Because the Jenkins home will be down-sized, Fergie will have to find a new home for his huge collection of memorabilia. He and Lydia plan to catalogue the contents of the collection and put it into safe storage so that the multitude of celebrity autographs will be protected from deterioration. Eventually, it will be inherited by his children.

Fergie's life has been an incredibly rich tapestry. As a young lad, he never could have imagined that he would enjoy the pride of success as a professional baseball pitcher, with all the adulation that such a career provides. He has fulfilled his dream of farming and raising high quality animals. He

Lydia and Fergie Jenkins

has the satisfaction of working to help those who have not been so fortunate in their lives. At the same time, he has known more sadness than one person should be expected to endure.

All of this has combined with a lifelong spiritual faith to create a man of exceptional strength. Fergie Jenkins is an example of the words written by the famous clergyman Peter Marshall - "Oaks grow strong in contrary winds and diamonds are made under pressure."

Ferguson Jenkins' long-time trainer and friend, Gene Dziadura summed up this unusual man's unusual career very neatly. He said "He played the game with dignity and grace. He continues to show this dignity and grace in his personal appearances, awards and generosity to others." That is a fitting tribute to the man who has accepted the good and the bad in life with natural courtesy.

A LIFETIME OF ACHIEVEMENT

1942   Ferguson Jenkins Jr. born December 13, in Chatham, Ontario

1959   First drawn to the attention of Phillies scout Gene Dziadura

1961-62   Athlete of the Year, Chatham Vocational School

1962   High School graduation and signing with the Philadelphia Phillies.

1962   Joined Williamsport, Pennsylvania Class A team

1962   Miami Marlins Class D

1962   Chattanooga Lookouts

1962   Buffalo Bisons Class AAA

1963   Little Rock Travellers

1963   Miami Marlins Class A

1963-64   Played winter ball in Managua, Nicaragua

1964   Sportsman of the Year, Chatham Chamber of Commerce

1965   February 13th - married to Anne Katherine Williams

1965-66   Played on All-Star team for Cayuga, Puerto Rico team

1965   Philadelphia Phillies

1966   Chicago Cubs

1966-67   Played winter ball in Dominican Republic

1967-68   Toured with the Harlem Globe Trotters

1967	Canadian Male Athlete of the Year
1968	Canadian Male Athlete of the Year
1971	Canadian Male Athlete of the Year
1971	Cy Young Award
1971	Pitches 100th career win in game against the Atlanta Braves
1971	City of Chatham erects a sign at its entrance reading "Welcome to Chatham - Home of Fergie Jenkins."
1972	Canadian Male Athlete of the Year
1972	Pitcher for National League All-Star Team
1972	Honorary member of Branch 421, Canadian Legion, Chatham
1972	Pitcher of the Year, Braves '400' Club, Eddie Glennon Gamboree
1974	Texas Rangers, American League
1974	American League Comeback Player of the Year
1974	Triple Crown Contender in the National League with 143.86 points. He had already been a three-time runner-up.
1974	Lou Marsh Trophy
1975	The Fergie Jenkins Trophy established by the Chatham Minor Baseball Organization for the Most Valuable Player In Chatham's baseball program.
1976	Boston Red Sox
1979	Member Order of Canada, Ottawa

1980	Charged with possession of drugs in Toronto
1982	Chicago Cubs
1984	Official retirement
1984	The Fergie Jenkins Community Service Award established by the Chatham Minor Baseball Organization, to be awarded to a member of the CMBO who has given 15 years of service to the organization
1984	Inducted into the Chatham Sports Hall of Fame
1987	Canadian Sports Hall of Fame, Calgary
1987	Canadian Baseball Hall of Fame, St. Marys, Ontario
1988	Married Mary-Anne Miller in Las Vegas
1991	Baseball Hall of Fame, Cooperstown, New York
1991	Sign at the entrance to Chatham changed to read "Welcome to Chatham - Home of Fergie Jenkins, Baseball's Hall of Famer"
1992	One of two first Canadians inducted International Afro-American Sports Hall of Fame and Gallery, Detroit
1992	Fergie Jenkins Bursary Award established to be awarded to a student-athlete in Chatham Kent.
1992	Chatham City Council declared an entrance street in the city to be named "Fergie Jenkins Way".
1992	Founding member Oklahoma Sports Museum, Guthrie, Oklahoma
1993	December, married to Lydia Farrington at Lakeview Ranch

1994	Pitching Coach for Chicago Cubs
1995	National League honorary pitching coach for All-Star team
1997	Inducted into the Ontario Sports Legends Hall of Fame at Pickering, Ontario
1997	Sports Celebrity Dinner in Grimsby, September 27th.
1999	The traditional baseball park at Rotary Park in Chatham renamed "Fergie Jenkins Field in Rotary Park."
2000	Sod-turning for Jenkins Field at Camp Maple Leaf on Pigeon Lake, Ontario
2000	Fergie Jenkins Foundation Inc., established.
2001	Inducted into the Walk of Fame in Toronto & Appointed Commissioner for the Canadian Baseball League
2002	They named a street after Fergie in Guthrie, OK called "Hubert "Geese" Ausbie & Fergie Jenkins Way"
2004	Inducted into the Texas Rangers Hall of Fame
2004	Awarded Honorary Doctrine of Law from McMaster University, Hamilton, Ontario
2006	Inducted into the Black Ice Hockey & Sports Hall of Fame, Dartmouth, Nova Scotia
2007	Appointed to the Minister's Advisors Committee on Sport
2007	Received the Order of Canada, May 4th, 2007
2007	Has donated close to a million dollars to charities through The Fergie Jenkins Foundation

Places Named for Fergie

1992	Chatham City Council renamed major street in the city Fergie Jenkins Way
1993	New playing field at Canadian Baseball Hall of Fame, St. Marys, Ontario
1999	Traditional ballpark at Rotary Park in Chatham renamed "Fergie Jenkins Field in Rotary Park."
2000	New ball field at Camp Maple Leaf, Pigeon Lake, Ontario Named Jenkins Field
2001	Original gymnasium at John McGregor School renamed Fergie Jenkins Auditorium

Author's Note

When Carl Kovacs first approached me to ask if I would write this book, I immediately said a firm "No!" Although I knew who Ferguson Jenkins was, I was not a baseball fan, and knew nothing at all about the rules of the game. It just didn't seem like my kind of writing.

Carl persisted, however, and eventually I started to do a little research. Then I met Fergie and had an opportunity to chat with him. Before long, I was caught up in Fergie's life and career. It has turned out to be a fascinating project. I hope readers will enjoy this true story as much as I have enjoyed writing it.

Many people deserve thanks for their part in the production of this book. First of all, to the members of the board of the Fergie Jenkins Foundation for deciding that there was a need for an updated biography of Ferguson Jenkins Jr. Thanks, too, to Carl Kovacs of the board for convincing me that I should be the one to write the book.

Thanks also to Gene Dziadura for his tremendous input into the content of the book. Gene spent considerable time on Father's Day, 2001 not just talking to me "on the record", but driving me around Chatham to see all the places that are most closely associated with Fergie. Although I had met and interviewed Fergie on a number of occasions by this time, this tour of his hometown brought his early life into perspective for me. Gene also agreed to read and edit the manuscript for this book. He took this responsibility very seriously, making some excellent suggestions and correcting my baseball terminology.

Thanks also to Carl McCoomb, curator of the Canadian Baseball Hall of Fame who took us around the HOF and provided more information and insight.

A great deal of information about Fergie's early life was provided by some of friends from his childhood and teenage years, including Dennis Steele, Ken Milburn, Bryan Eaton, Casey Maynard, Billy Atkinson and Mike Bennett. Reminiscences of the Chatham All-Stars was provided by Don Tavron, Segasta Harding and Horace Chase. Thanks to Sharon and Fred Oldfield for information about sports cards. It was a rare treat to talk to Bill "Space Man" Lee about the Buffalo Head Gang. He is an unforgettable character.

Also, thanks to Doug Kay, fund-raising co-ordinator of Hamilton East Community Services for providing information about and photos taken at Camp Maple Leaf.

I also wish to thank Brian Masschaele who introduced me to the books by William Humber which provided interesting insight into the history of baseball in Canada.

I also wish to thank Tony Riviera, founder and chairman of the board of the Canadian Baseball League for his insight into Fergie's new role in the world of baseball.

Not to be forgotten are Des Morris and his team at Peninsula Press who designed and produced this book. They have been a pleasure to work with.

Special thanks to my husband Jim who has accompanied me and supported me all along the way. I often had to call upon his lifelong love of baseball to answer simple questions and explain some of the fine points of The Game.

Dorothy Turcotte

Bibliography

Chieger, Bob. *The Cubbies. Quotations on the Chicago Cubs.* Atheneum, New York, 1987.

Humber, William. *Cheering for the Home Team. The Story of Baseball in Canada.* The Boston Mills Press, Erin, Ontario. 1983.

Humber, William. *Diamonds of the North. A Concise History of Baseball in Canada.* Oxford University Press, Toronto, 1995.

Jenkins, Ferguson. *Like Nobody Else. The Fergie Jenkins Story.* As told to George Vass. Henry Regnery Company, Chicago. 1973.

Miller, Marvin. *A Whole Different Ball Game; The Sport and Business of Baseball.* A Birch Lane Press Book, Secaucus, New Jersey, 1991.

Minteer, Robert L. *Pitching's Triple Crown Contenders.* Third Millennium Publishing, Tempe, Arizona, 2000.

Morgan, Joe. *Baseball for Dummies.* With Richard Lally, 2nd edition. IDG Books Worldwide Inc., Foster City, CA. 2000.

Pashko, Stanley. *Ferguson Jenkins.* The Quiet Winner. G.P. Putnam's Sons, New York. 1975

Reidenbaugh, Lowell. *Baseball's Hall of Fame; Coopertown, Where the Legends Live Forever.* Random House Value Publishing Inc., Avenel, N.J., 1994

Ryan, Nolan, and Herskowitz, Mickey. *Kings of the Hill An Irreverent Look at the Men on the Mound.,* HarperCollins, New York, NY., 1992

Smith, Ron. *The Ballpark Book,* The Sporting News, St. Louis, MO., 2000

Index

"A LIFETIME OF MEMORIES"

Fergie's Diamond Memories

Lydia - Fergie - Prince

Fergie and his love for the outdoors

*Fergie at bat
with the Cubs*

*Fergie receiving a watch for
Player of the Month from Paul Shivers*

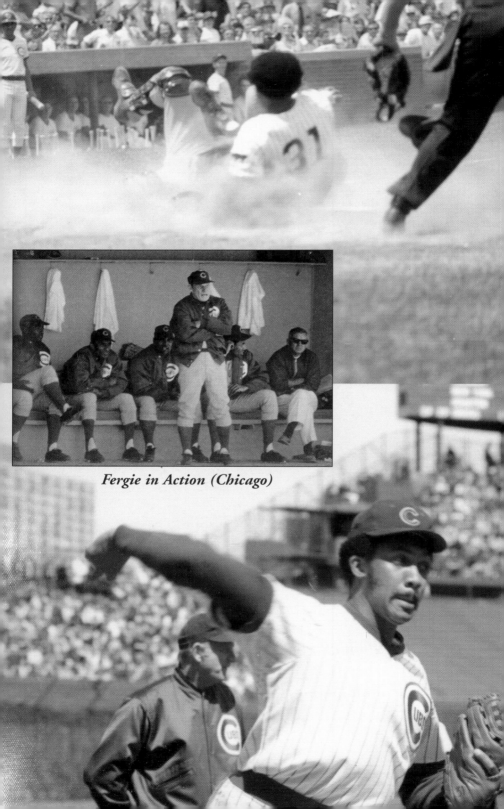

Fergie in Action (Chicago)

Fergie as a Globetrotter 1967-69

PHILLIES
1966 ROOKIE STARS

FERGUSON JENKINS p   BILL SORRELL 1b-of

FERGIE
JENKINS
CHICAGO CUBS
PITCHER

CUBS

Fergie Jenkins PITCHER

Fergie with the Texas Rangers

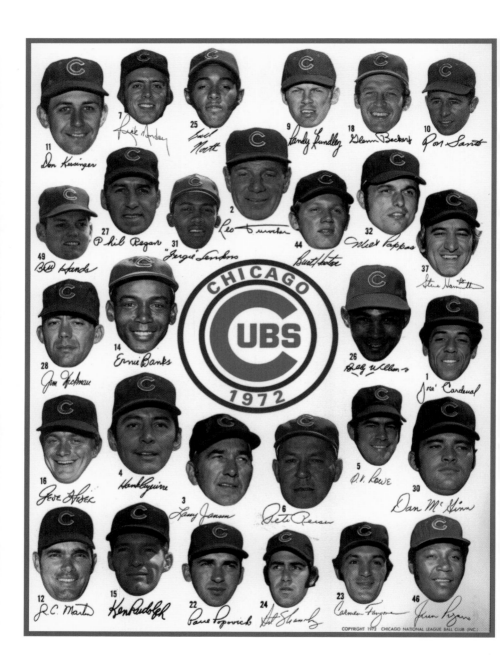

TEXAS RangerS
1974
Arlington Stadium

FERGUSON JENKINS

- HALL OF FAME 1991
- COMEBACK PLAYER OF THE YEAR 1974
- CY YOUNG AWARD WINNER 1971
- 'SPORTING NEWS' PLAYER OF THE YEAR 1968
- 49 CAREER SHUTOUTS
- 284 TOTAL WINS
- 3,192 STRIKE OUTS
- 997 WALKS
- 267 CAREER COMPLETE GAMES

Come Back Player of the Year - 1974

Sports Illustrated

AUGUST 30, 1971   60 CENTS

HERE COME
THE CUBS

Ferguson Jenkins
wins his 20th

Fergie and Lydia Jenkins, Gene & Marie Dziadura

Fergie and the fab four, Carl Kovacs,
Gene Dziadura, John Oddi, Peter Warkentin

Lydia in a Jay uniform with grandson Kaleb

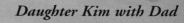

Daughter Kim with Dad

Mac Voisin and Fergie Jenkins at the M&M Crohns & Colitis Celebrity Golf Classic July 2002

Photo courtesy of M&M Meat Shops Ltd.

Artist Terry Quirk from the UK sketched this piece for the 2001 Celebrity Event

#31 FERGIE JENKINS
~H.O.F. - 91~

Actor Sean McCann with the Niagara Regional Police at the Four Points Sheraton

Fergie with his Walk of Fame Star & famous cowboy hat

At Rockway Glen the first Annual Charity Classic

Johnny Bower, Scott Bullet JoAnne Malar, Bob Gibson, Bobby Bell, Bert Campaneris at the 1999 Charity Golf Tournament